**Pat Cummins** is captain of the Australian Men's Test and One Day International cricket teams, and was named 2023 ICC Cricketer of the Year. He has been pivotal in re-shaping team culture and leading them to global success across all formats of the game. He aligns himself with organisations dedicated to creating lasting impact and supports initiatives involving education, sustainability, First Nations communities and health.

Pat lives in Sydney with his wife, Becky, and their son, Albie.

# TESTED

## PAT CUMMINS

HarperCollins*Publishers*

Aboriginal and Torres Strait Islander people are respectfully advised that *Tested* contains descriptions, images and names of people now deceased.

Ben McKelvey worked as a journalist in Sydney and abroad, embedded with the ADF in Iraq and East Timor, and independently in Afghanistan, Syria and Iran. He is the author or co-author of six books and has won an Indie Book Award and a NiB Military History Award, and been shortlisted in the Victorian Premier's Literary Awards, Queensland Premier's Literary Awards, Australian Book Industry Awards, the National Biography Award and more.

**HarperCollins***Publishers*
Australia • Brazil • Canada • France • Germany • Holland • India
Italy • Japan • Mexico • New Zealand • Poland • Spain • Sweden
Switzerland • United Kingdom • United States of America

HarperCollins acknowledges the Traditional Custodians
of the lands upon which we live and work, and pays respect
to Elders past and present.

First published on Gadigal Country in Australia in 2024
by HarperCollins*Publishers* Australia Pty Limited
ABN 36 009 913 517
harpercollins.com.au

A catalogue record for this book is available from the National Library of Australia

ISBN 978 1 4607 6491 6 (paperback)
ISBN 978 1 4607 1685 4 (ebook)
ISBN 978 1 4607 3041 6 (audiobook)

Cover design by Darren Holt, HarperCollins Design Studio
Back cover image by Hugh Stewart
Typeset in Adobe Garamond Pro by Kirby Jones
Printed and bound in Australia by McPherson's Printing Group

MIX
Paper from
responsible sources
FSC
www.fsc.org   FSC® C001695

*For Mum*

*I know you would hate the attention and credit for this.*
*But you taught me that everyone has a story, and to stay*
*curious enough to find out what it is.*
*You were tested more than anyone should be.*
*You showed me the meaning of resolve every single day*
*that you stayed strong, for us.*

# CONTENTS

# Introduction

WHEN THE CALL CAME THROUGH TELLING ME THAT I was being considered to become the next Australian Test captain, my initial thought was *Please, not now.* It was November 2021, and I was in quarantine on the Gold Coast with most of the Australian team, the English side, and also my wife, Becky, and our baby son, Albie. It felt like everything was happening all at once.

Albie had been born a month earlier and, after only a handful of days together, I had to fly out for the T20 World Cup in the United Arab Emirates. We won that tournament on 14 November, then flew back to Australia and entered quarantine ready for a quick turnaround for an Ashes series scheduled to start at the Gabba on 8 December.

I was so appreciative that Becky and Albie were allowed to enter quarantine with me, because I desperately wanted to spend time with them away from cricket and crowds. I wanted the three of us to get away from the world – and frankly, I wanted to start to learn to be a dad and to pull my weight in this new family.

Then, a few days into the quarantine, the phone rang. It was our high-performance coach telling me that Tim Paine was being removed as captain of the Test team, and that the board wanted me and Steve Smith to present to the Cricket Australia selection panel, making our cases to replace him.

*Please, not now.*

I firmly believe that everyone has the capacity to start from square one on anything, if they're given the space to do so. Now I found myself at square one being a dad and potentially Test captain. I was already working to capacity on one thing, and along came another. I'd also had in my head that I would learn how to be a dad, a leader within the team too, and then, maybe later, I'd be ready to be captain. Those weren't the only reasons I was reticent, though, nor – if I were being honest – the primary reasons. The truth was, I didn't feel prepared.

I'd recently captained New South Wales in a handful of one-day matches, but before that I hadn't captained a side since I was fifteen. I hadn't even really thought that much about being the captain, even though I'd been a vice-captain for some time. I was a bowler, after all; there hadn't been a bowler who'd captained the Test team for generations.

Those were my initial thoughts. It wasn't until I started to put a presentation together for the selection panel that my mind changed, wholly and fully. I found I had strong feelings about what kind of captain I'd want to be and what kind of team I'd like to lead. I wanted to empower the other players and to collaborate with them. I wanted to foster an environment of respect, and I wanted the team to be role models for young players, while being authentic and honest. I wanted the team to be curious, to help others and to strive for joy. I also just wanted us to have a lot of fun.

I put some declarative quotes in a presentation I felt was itself authentic and honest. 'Being a cricketer is part of life, it doesn't define me.' And 'All problems can be solved.'

I still refer to that document now, checking my outcomes against my goals as a captain.

In putting that presentation together, I realised I had more leadership experience than I'd imagined, both on and off the pitch. I felt like I knew my own style and perspective.

My life had been full in the past few years, and I'd changed. In my youth I'd sometimes been passive and dogmatic, but I felt I was now less so. I'd grabbed life with both hands. I'd had to – I'd become engaged to the love of my life and welcomed a son into the world. My mum had also been given the devastating information that the cancer that had started in her breast had spread to her brain; she would not go into remission.

Mum always used to tell me that I was able to rise to any new challenge, even though I might not believe it myself.

I began to think this was as good a time as any for me to be captain – the best time, really, because my mum and dad could watch it happen. Opportunities are what we make of them, and I wanted to make this one count.

When I presented to the board, I was excited and hopeful but also very comfortable with where I was in that stage in my life and totally okay with not being captain. There was a perception – in the wake of Tim Paine's removal as captain, and with the ball-tampering scandal still hanging over the team – that this was somehow a foreboding and wary time for us. But I didn't see it that way. We'd just won the T20 World Cup, and I believed we were a good team of great blokes in an excellent position to win a home Ashes series.

It was announced at the end of November that I'd be taking on the mantle. Less than a fortnight later, I was out in the middle, wearing the baggy green and the blazer, ready for the toss for the first Ashes Test. Becky, Mum and Dad watched on from home (in a flood of tears).

During that Ashes series I spent a lot of time thinking about leadership. I've spent a lot of time thinking about it since, too. I've wondered at what point I became ready to take on the captaincy, and how I got to that point of readiness. I haven't been able to identify the exact moment, but I now understand what I needed to learn get there. What would separate eighteen-year-old me, ready to play my first Test match, from the now twenty-eight-year-old me, ready to lead a Test team?

I think what I developed in those ten years was resolve.

Resolve is the drive to keep going, the wisdom to know where to focus your energies, and the fortitude to fight against the obstacles that you find along the way. It's not necessarily relentlessness, ruthlessness or bloody-mindedness; it's a steady hand, a deft touch and the ability to keep your head when everyone around you is losing theirs. Resolve is physical, emotional and moral courage born of a knowledge of yourself.

It is hard to describe but easy to recognise, and when I see it in people, from any field and in my personal life, I'm always interested in where they first acquired theirs.

I find the answers to my probing are varied, but one truth always comes through: resolve emerges from experience.

Sometimes that experience is slow and incremental, but often it comes in a flash. There are moments in our lives that we can clearly point to when we were one person before and another person after.

Such moments are not often sought out, and many times they occur in circumstances that you wouldn't wish upon your worst enemy, but often these moments are the making of us. They are the crucible for the resolve we will use for the next stage of life, the next challenge, the next obstacle.

I've always been fascinated by those moments, and I've long been interested in writing a book. But when I sat down with publishers or agents, they'd suggest I work on a biography or a tour diary or something like that. I've never wanted to do that. Perhaps one day it might excite me to work on that sort of book, but at this point in my life I wanted to write something different.

I didn't want to focus on myself, as I might with a memoir. I wanted to learn. I wanted to sit down with people from varied fields who'd gone through exceptional experiences and thrived afterwards. I wanted to speak with people who'd been tested in challenges that were grand and also personal, and I wanted to learn from them. I was excited about the prospect of writing a book like that, but I thought I'd need a bit of help from someone with different experiences to mine. There is a lot of hard-earned wisdom out there in the world and I wanted to capture some.

I'd met the author and journalist Ben Mckelvey a few years earlier, when he was profiling me for a magazine. Since then I'd picked up a couple of his biographies and his book about the activities of Australia's special forces in Afghanistan. The book that most made me want to work with Ben, though, was his memoir, *A Scar Is Also Skin*. It tells the story of some of Ben's own difficult moments, which came after he suffered an aphasic stroke – meaning he lost the ability to read and write for some months – and a heart attack while he was in his twenties. It was while he was recovering from those that he developed the insight he'd need for his career as an author. That brush with death also spurred him to head off and cover the story he really wanted to: the Iraq War.

Ben and I put together an ambitious wish list of accomplished people I might speak to about their testing moments, their leadership journeys, who I wanted to understand and learn from.

We began with an interview centred on a monumental Australian sporting moment: with John Bertrand, skipper of *Australia II*, the racing yacht that won the 1983 America's Cup, breaking an American winning streak that went back to the time of the US Civil War. From John I learned how radical change like the kind I hoped to create in my team can't be demanded, it needs to be earned – often after a long period of disappointment and failure.

Perhaps the most moving interview was with Professor Richard Scolyer, who, along with his colleague Professor Georgina Long, are the 2024 Australians of the Year. Rich was one of the world's preeminent cancer researchers when he was diagnosed with what had previously been considered an untreatable brain cancer. Rich turned his tragedy into opportunity, subjecting himself to an experimental treatment developed with Professor Long and their colleagues. He welcomed me into his home, and as I sat at his dinner table, alongside his wife and son, I was taken back to my mum's own battle with cancer. I swelled with pride and hope as I sat with a man who, amid his own life-and-death battle, still chose to be on the front lines of medical research.

I marveled at the resilience Rich has, as I had at Mum's resilience too. In the face of fear and incredible trial, Rich maintained his life's mission, his personal values and his drive. He has a clarity of purpose, a drive to work towards that purpose and the bravery to keep going when obstacles large or small arrive.

It was my privilege to sit down with Julia Gillard, who showed me a very different side to the one I'd seen on television while she was the prime minister of Australia.

My next interview was with John Moriarty, a legend of Australian soccer and the first Indigenous man to be selected for the national side. He's also an artist, a political activist and a survivor of the Stolen Generations. I know him quite well, but I still felt nervous on my way to his house. When John told his story, though, with his wife, Ros, next to him, I felt increasingly inspired. He has an incredible story – really, it's part of Australia's national story – and I felt privileged to hear it from him.

Dennis Lillee has been one of the most important people in my cricketing career, spending a lot of time with me as I was trying to find a sustainable bowling action when I was suffering through injury after injury. We spoke about his approach and philosophies as a coach, though I'll admit we spent most of our time discussing the World Series Cricket competition, and his involvement in the professionalisation of the game.

Next we sat down with a man who is giving back in a very different way. Full of love and with the biggest heart, Shaun Christie-David has built a successful and unique restaurant and catering company with a bottom line that isn't money but social capital.

I couldn't wait for the next interview, with long-distance runner Nedd Brockmann. Sitting in my living room, with Albie running about in the kitchen behind us, Nedd explained what keeps him going when the road ahead seems endless. When he described his most painful moments as also his most glorious, it pumped me up as well.

I'd previously met with bestselling British author Elizabeth Day in London to record an episode of her podcast *How to Fail*, but for this book we spoke in a triangular interview, with me in India, Ben in Sydney and Elizabeth in

London. At this point almost everyone in the world knows that meeting over Teams or Zoom can often create a stilted conversation, but Elizabeth was warm and exceptionally open. I felt I'd genuinely shared an experience with her when we talked about how her personal and professional failures helped her become the success she is today.

Speaking of success stories, I also sat down with media titan, Bollywood producer and philanthropist Ronnie Screwvala, who agreed to meet me while I was on tour in Mumbai so we could speak about persistence, vision and serendipity.

Rob Sitch and I spoke about his classic Australian films *The Castle* and *The Dish* as well as the TV series *Utopia* and *The Hollowmen*. I wanted to speak to this father of five about how he continues to achieve so much, and I discovered how the privilege of being a dad made him a better creator.

I garnered something different from each person I spoke with, but for my last conversation I wanted to discuss partnership with my beautiful wife, Becky. This ended up being the hardest interview to land.

We had planned to have a conversation and work on the chapter for this book while we were in the West Indies for the T20 World Cup, but our attempts to chat were frequently hijacked by our jet-lagged two-year-old, and we had to put those plans on the backburner when we were presented with our own life-changing experience: discovering that we would soon be welcoming a second child into the world.

Becky and Albie went on to the United Kingdom to spend time with her parents, and I joined them after the competition ended. There, Becky and I finally managed to carve out a couple of child-free hours at her mum's place. It was a wonderful but strange experience to formally investigate the moments that have tested us together. That interview made me realise how much has happened in my life – in my playing career, and in my roles as a husband, dad, brother and son – and how much my life has changed because of those testing moments. It also made me realise how important having people like Becky and Albie and my parents has been to ensure that each change is positive.

*

I learned a lot while writing and researching this book. I'm so grateful for the conversations I had with the unique and brilliant team of leaders featured in these pages. I thank them for their generosity and time but especially for trusting in the experiment of this book. Their stories, their openness and frankness have blown me away.

In my interview with Elizabeth Day, she talked about embracing the opportunities failure brings you. I didn't know what to expect when I started the process of making this book. I'd hoped not to fail. I was definitely out of my comfort zone. It was much harder than I had anticipated, but with that challenge came the wisdom I had hoped for when I embarked on this project. Just not in the way I expected.

In gaining understanding of success and failure, I also gained a better understanding of myself, and how my own resolve – in those moments where I've been tested and in those big and small decisions across my life – has helped me as a player, a captain and a man.

My hope for this book, in sharing the stories of these extraordinary people and my own leadership journey, is that it reinforces for you, too, the power of your own resolve in the face of opportunity, complication and challenge.

After all, there's always another test.

# 1

## The impossible is only possible when all other options have been exhausted

*A conversation with John Bertrand*

THE FAMED SKIPPER OF THE 1983 AMERICA'S CUP-winning boat, *Australia II*, and former Swimming Australia president, John Bertrand is an analytical man. In his youth he studied Engineering at university; later he launched a company on the Nasdaq and became a university vice-chancellor professorial fellow.

John understands the science of sport: the physics and biodynamics, statistics and probabilities. He also understands the emotional and esoteric parts, which he says are just as important. He understands that sport is undertaken by humans, not machines, with our emotions able to hinder or enhance our performance.

'You have to have emotion,' John said. 'To do well in anything – anything at all – you've got to have passion and drive. And you've got to have luck, too. It's very, very important.'

\*

I interviewed John Bertrand remotely, as I was in India playing in the IPL when our interview was scheduled. John had presented to a leadership group Mitchell Marsh is part of, and Marshy had been totally inspired and told me I had to speak to John. When we connected, I saw a man who seemed far younger than his seventy-seven years, and when we started speaking about his childhood, he seemed even younger again.

'My first piece of luck,' John told me, 'was that Mum and Dad rented a house at Chelsea, south of Melbourne, meaning my brother and I could climb over the side fence of our house and we'd be on the beach on Port Phillip Bay. That meant my brother and I would be mucking around in boats, and I became fascinated with this strange sport of sailing.'

John started competing in the sport at a very young age, first sailing Sabot dinghies, a popular craft for young sailors, before flourishing as a club racer. He said that at the time he competed because he loved it, not because he could see some pot of gold at the end of the rainbow. 'My dream wasn't to win the America's Cup or anything – I just loved watching the bubbles go past. I just loved sailing and the dream of it all.'

He proved to be an exceptional competitor, becoming the national dinghy champion and then being picked for the Australian 1972 and 1976 Olympic Games teams. He competed in the Finn Class, known as the most gruelling of the Olympic sailing classes, in which competitors sail single-handed dinghies that require tactical prowess and athleticism. In 1972, John came fourth, and in 1976 he did one better, finding himself on the podium.

Sailing is one of the original Olympic sports, but Olympic sailing is not the pinnacle of the sport. Like cycling's Tour de France and motorsport's Formula 1, sailing has a blue-ribbon event that exists in a different category to all other competition in the sport; an event where human and mechanical innovation progress together, and where history is made in the most dramatic fashion. This is the America's Cup, which is unlike the Tour de France and F1 racing in that the competitors and the craft designers and fabricators are often one and the same.

John competed in his first America's Cup the year he graduated from Monash University with a Mechanical Engineering honours degree. Then competing as a twenty-two-year-old, John was a port trimmer – essentially a crew member who gauges and predicts wind and adjusts sails accordingly – for Frank Packer's boat, *Gretel II*, incidentally the first keel boat John had ever set foot on.

The dynamics of America's Cup racing totally engrossed John. Going back to the F1 comparison, it was the difference between driving a production model vehicle and a custom-built race car. 'Aerodynamics was always a fascination for me,' he said, 'and I dreamed in that space.'

After that 1970 campaign, John also dreamed of one day leading an America's Cup campaign as the Australian skipper. He moved to the United States so he could complete a Master of Science in Naval Architecture at the Massachusetts

Institute of Technology (MIT), one of the most famous science and technology universities in the world. His thesis was: 'The Optimum Angle of Attack of America's Cup Sails.'

John wanted to be the skipper and also win the Cup – which, for a non-American then, was arguably the most outlandish dream in sports. Since the competition's foundation in 1851, the Americans had always won the race, thanks in no small part to the money America's captains of industry had thrown at it. The surnames of the country's team owners were a who's who of American industry, such as Forbes, Vanderbilt, Morgan and Sears. Every America's Cup final contest had been between two teams: a defender – the team that formerly won the Cup – and a challenger. By the time John started competing in the Cup there had been challengers from the United Kingdom, Canada, Australia, Ireland and France, and the challenger had never won. The idea of winning the Cup as a challenger was called the 'Everest of sporting endeavours', although climbers had actually crested that summit.

Since 1962, the Australian media baron Frank Packer, Kerry's father and James's grandfather, had poured millions into attempts to unseat the Americans for the Royal Sydney Yacht Squadron. He never managed it. After the 1970 loss, he announced, 'This is the last you will hear from me, good luck.'

The challenge was then taken up by a new Australian billionaire, Alan Bond, for the Royal Perth Yacht Club. Later in life, Bond was proved to have undertaken corrupt business practices, and he served four years in jail – but while he was challenging the Americans in the Cup, he was one of Australia's richest and most successful men.

Bond's first tilt at the Cup was in 1974, with John again on the yacht as a crew member and assistant designer. This boat, *Southern Cross*, didn't win one race in the best-of-seven final series. Six years later, John was on Bond's new yacht, *Australia*, when it lost the final series 4–1. He told me, 'The Americans are highly competitive people and are not in the business of losing. They'll eat their grandmother if that's what's required to win. We went through the school of hard knocks [losing three Cup campaigns] and learned a lot by being beaten up by the Yanks.'

John had suspected during the 1980 campaign that Alan Bond was using that year as a 'holding action', limiting the budget in a campaign that was primarily a stepping stone towards the main tilt in 1983. John's suspicions were confirmed when Bond jumped aboard *Australia* just after the team had lost the final race and was coming into the harbour at Newport, New York. 'Don't worry, boys,' John recalled Bond saying. 'That was great, we gave it our best shot ... I have decided that we are coming back in 1983 with a major challenge. We'll have the budget and the boat. And we are going to win the America's Cup.'

Alan Bond made another announcement: the next boat would be captained by John Bertrand.

\*

John said one important factor in his team's 1983 America's Cup campaign was a very strong organisational structure. And it's not just John who has said that, either: the famed thinker and theorist Edward de Bono, who coined the phrase 'lateral thinking', used that Cup campaign as a model when describing one of his organisational theories.

Six Thinking Hats is a theory made famous by a book of the same name. In it, De Bono argues that humans should use varied approaches when considering a problem, as the discordant thinking can turbo-charge understanding and progress. De Bono's book champions small group work, ideally with each participant representing one of the ways of thinking detailed in the theory while assuming a role that has a unique mindset and responsibility. When explaining the concept to me, John cited the construction of the Trans-Siberian Railway as an example, with Imperial Russia using small pods of diverse engineers to attack each problem instead of relying on a monolithic, top-down approach. He also cited Lockheed Martin's Advanced Development Programs – better known as the Skunk Works – which have deliberately used small teams with varied skills and experience to develop such marvels such as the SR-71 Blackbird plane.

Of the six different mindsets and responsibilities, one of the most powerful, according to de Bono, is the Black Hat: a thinker who must assess risks, difficulties, problems and opportunities. This is the hat that, in de Bono's analysis, John wore in the 1983 America's Cup campaign. The theorist may describe this hat as the most powerful, but that does not mean it is the most important. In this case, it's arguable that the Green Hat is just as important. 'The Green Hat is the out-there, crazy thinker,' said John. 'They have the most radical ideas, and perhaps for every ten ideas, one could be implemented.'

The Green Hat thinker in that Cup campaign was the boat's designer, Ben Lexcen. John described him as 'Australia's da Vinci'. Coming from a broken and difficult home in country New South Wales, Lexcen had no formal schooling except his three years at Boys' Town, a school hosting orphans as well as children with significant behavioural issues. He trained for a while as a locomotive fitter and turner, before he found he had a love and aptitude for sailing. Like John, Lexcen competed as a sailor, but it was as a marine architect that he really excelled. By the early eighties, Lexcen had designed boats for various companies and individuals, including Alan Bond, but he wasn't known as a scientific and mathematical designer, unlike most America's Cup boat designers.

When Bond stood on the deck of *Australia* after losing in 1980 and announced that John Bertrand would be the skipper of the 1983 America's Cup tilt, he also announced that Ben Lexcen would design his new boat, which would end up being called *Australia II*. Lexcen would prove to be an exemplary Green Hat thinker, truly going beyond the bounds of what had been imagined before in the design of twelve-metre yachts.

With a mandate for radical thought, Lexcen went to the state-of-the-art Netherlands Ship Model Basin at

Wageningen. Using early versions of computer modelling, he worked on potential designs. He came back to Perth with a number of suggestions, including an all-Kevlar running rigging and a lightweight carbon fibre boom, and perhaps the most conceptually unusual and famous design element in the history of yacht racing: a winged keel.

A boat's keel is usually a flat blade that sticks down into the water from the bottom, providing two functions: preventing the boat from being blown sideways by the wind, and holding the ballast that keeps the boat right side up. Lexcen's designs suggested essentially an upside-down keel that would scythe into the water and then open up like wings at the bottom. The hope was that the keel would put the ballast lower in the boat, and that this might improve stability without creating extra drag. All in all, that might mean more speed, especially in rough waters.

Might. Could. This boat, with its wild innovations, would take a vast amount of resources and time to build, and it was far from sure to be a fast racing boat. John told me, 'I was really concerned when the winged keel was unveiled by Benny. I thought, *Just give me some normal equipment and I'll get the job done.* Bondy was very much about taking the risk, though.' Bond, someone who understood risk and was comfortable with it – a little too comfortable, as it would later turn out – was the man making the decisions, so onward they went with Lexcen's plans.

The team that was to race the yacht was also to build the yacht, so John and his team took to building what would become *Australia II*, from skeleton to rigging, in a warehouse in Perth. After they launched the boat, John said he realised the brilliance of Ben Lexcen and his design.

At MIT, a professor had told John that 'until you can put a problem into numbers, you'll never be able to solve it', and he'd taken this advice to heart. But Lexcen tested that wisdom. He was a designer but not an engineer. He was a scientist but not an educated one. He'd been designing boats for years, but in each case he'd primarily designed by feel, liking especially to contemplate designs in nature that he thought could be taken into the field of yacht construction.

John was wary of people who said that they might be able to act without explaining their actions. Like any good mathematician, John believed you must show your workings. In the 1983 campaign, however, he found another way of thinking. 'Benny was unfettered,' John said of his barely educated designer. 'Alan Bond let him think outside the box and have no one laugh at him, and he came up with some truly over-the-horizon thinking. [I discovered that] intuitive decision-making, gut feel is extremely powerful.'

John said the radical nature of Lexcen's design ended up informing a lot of the culture of that campaign, because it changed John's thinking. That time taught him how monumentally difficult endeavours might be attempted and achieved: with total ambition and blue-sky thinking. He says he achieved that ambition and that thinking by imagining a future that was undoubtedly going to be better, faster, smarter. 'You get an improvement in performance every four years – one hundred metre sprint or whatever, doesn't matter – but the interesting thing about the Olympic movement is that over twenty years you have a quantum leap in every discipline. The world records in one twenty-year period are all smashed. All we know [is that] in twenty years' time the game will have progressed a lot. History tells us that. We said, "Let's try to get there faster than anyone else."'

John says that over-the-horizon thinking is a useful way of approaching a seemingly impossible task, and in that campaign it was also a way to create excitement, enthusiasm and a sense of possibility in a team that had experienced so much defeat. It worked on the team then, and it still works on him now. 'I still get excited listening to myself even now. That's not normal,' the seventy-seven-year-old said with a laugh. 'If you ever feel screwed up, Pat, don't worry about it. I've never met a world champion who isn't abnormal in some way. To get out of bed and do extraordinary things, you need to be like that.'

According to John, as a leader you need to have ambition beyond what seems to be possible. You need to have an eye on the immediate task but also what's over the horizon. 'You have to have vision to succeed, and that vision has to be exciting.'

Vision is a word that I found came up often when chatting to the leaders in this book. When everything was going awry, it's vision that centred them and gave them solid ground to return to. We try to hold to a vision too, in the Test team, which I'll come back to later.

When I was talking to John about hats, I thought about our own team too. I wanted our team to be an environment in which everyone could be themselves, could be free to work under the hat that they naturally aligned with. It's good to have a mix of people in the team, and that they all feel confident to throw ideas out or challenge us on existing ideas – especially the young guys, who aren't as burdened by the last ten years of how things have always been done.

I hadn't thought of about hats before speaking with John, but I've always found you do get a natural mix of personalities in any group, as long as you let people's personalities play out. In any group of ten people (whether mates, a team, or both) you're likely to have four to five who are fine as they are, a few who give you an idea a minute, and a few who gravitate towards being contrary. If you have any voids in the leadership roles, someone will inevitably fill them.

When we're doing team selection it's of course skills-based rather than focusing on leadership attributes. We have our experienced types like Usman Khawaja and Alex Carey who are happy to go about their work relatively quietly; who can have anything thrown their way and you know they'll deal with it. In the green hats, we can rely on guys like Steve Smith and Marnus Labuschagne – who think about cricket 24/7 – to throw a lot of great ideas and tactics and strategies our way. The bowlers Josh Hazlewood, Mitchell Starc and Nathan Lyon are rock-solid consistent personalities – great guys with pretty good radars for anyone getting too big for their boots, who might need to get pulled back in line. Then there are guys like Travis Head and Mitchell Marsh who are natural circuit-breakers – when the tension gets high, they know how to defuse the room and bring the team together.

It's one thing to make sure those people are in your team, though, and another to foster that spirit where everyone feels confident to speak up. So it was with John Bertrand and his team. With a vision and a mindset that weren't just business as usual, inspired by a boat that wasn't just business as usual, John said he felt like the team had a licence to break the mould and to think and train differently. That training involved running and calisthenics – not something commonly done by America's Cup yachtsmen in the early eighties – and meditation, mindfulness and visualisation. This kind of mental training is now pretty standard in high-performance sports, as it's scientifically proven to improve concentration and confidence, but back then it was about as derided as sunscreen and recycling.

With John's licence, however, he did it, hoping to instil in the team a calmness, a coolness and a belief that they could actually win the Cup. He thought those ideas would be essential so they – and he – wouldn't be crushed under the weight of expectation and history, and by the idea that failure was inevitable.

*

There had never been more interest in an America's Cup final than in 1983. When John and his team arrived in Newport,

Rhode Island, to take on the defending champion, the New York Yacht Club's *Liberty*, they brought an unprecedented number of media and fans.

In the challengers' series, *Australia II* had blown the competition away. These performances had created intense public interest in the Australian team, and even more interest had built as to what was under their boat. Coming into the finals, no one outside the team had seen *Australia II*'s keel, as it had been wrapped with a covering every time the boat was out of the water. Tongues were wagging. There was intense speculation over whether this Australian challenger might be able to finally accomplish something that had been attempted so many times.

But after the first two races in the best-of-seven competition against *Liberty*, it looked as though all of the raised expectations and hopes for *Australia II* had been for nothing. In both of those races, the Australian boat had suffered different catastrophic equipment failures. *Australia II* managed to win the third race, but after the Americans won the fourth, few believed that – even with a fast boat and luck in their favour – the Australians would be able to beat the Americans three times consecutively. Then *Australia II* did win the fifth race. In doing so they made history, as no challenger had ever pushed the Americans to a sixth race. Which the Australians also won.

In the seventh race, though, they fell behind. And then they fell behind even more. In fact, *Australia II* fell so far behind that the commentators started announcing that the 132-year reign of the United States would be extended.

Then something happened. The American skipper Dennis Conner made a small mistake, and John Bertrand and his team started sailing their boat 'as close to perfection' as he'd ever known a boat to be sailed. He told me the boat collectively elevated into a flow state, and that his team became so tight and so close that they were also on 'autopilot'. There was no fear, no doubt, just performance. In his mind, John went back to his childhood and his simple love of sailing. He was in the final race of the America's Cup, going through a life-defining moment – for better or for worse – yet he managed to be the boy who just liked watching the bubbles go past. He was, again, just in the dream of it all.

*Australia II* blew across the line forty-one seconds ahead of *Liberty*. A cannon fired, and Australian sporting history was made.

Mayhem followed. The win was a moment of complete national rapture for Australia, best exemplified by the image of Prime Minister Bob Hawke, wearing a white blazer emblazoned with Australian flags and 'Australia' repeated dozens of times. At the Royal Perth Yacht Club in the early hours of the Australian morning, Hawke spoke the immortal words: 'Any boss who sacks anyone for not turning up today is a bum.'

John Bertrand was momentarily one of Australia's most famous men, as was Ben Lexcen, who died five years later at age fifty-one.

John kept racing yachts, but never again in the America's Cup, leaving another Australian skipper to try to defend the Cup in Perth in 1987. It was won by the American yacht *Stars & Stripes 87.* John says that he had conquered his Everest in 1983 and, like Sir Edmund Hillary before him, he didn't feel the need to go back.

\*

When I interviewed John, I was in India captaining the Sunrisers Hyderabad. I love playing in India, especially enjoying the passion that the games are played with. There's excitement on and off the pitch, but in the IPL season – like on every tour we have these days – there are periods in which your energy dips. Modern cricketers play a lot of cricket, and while each tournament, tour and Test is exciting, collectively they do catch up with us. We can miss home, our families and our routines. All of us, in those moments of lagging energy, remind ourselves how lucky we are to play cricket professionally and that the time we can do so is limited. Before we know it, we will no longer be asked to play. Not professionally, anyway.

There is use in finding something new and exciting about the way cricket is being played. It can bring a new energy to tired minds and tired legs. The season that I interviewed John, I also took a lot away from just how many runs were scored. In one of our matches there was an aggregate score of 549 runs for a run rate per over of nearly thirty, with

Travis Head smashing a century in forty balls. That knock and that match were fairly mind-blowing to me. It wasn't the only match with incredibly aggressive batting, either.

At times that IPL season, I felt like we were getting a preview of what cricket might be in the future. Could the bat become even more dominant in all forms of the game, and could we see even more fours and sixes? I think it could. Thankfully I'll probably be out of the sport by the time things get really out of hand, but it's an exciting and tantalising prospect that kept me energised throughout that season.

One of the things that really impressed me about John is that he didn't just look at the future as a place the game would naturally progress towards. He knew the sport was going to evolve and asked, 'So how do we fast-track that?' He approached the problems from a different angle, and when he worked on a problem he was all in.

When I started playing organised age cricket in under-fifteens or -seventeens, I'd look at the boys around me and think, *They have two arms, two legs like me. What makes them so special? I'll show them.* Perhaps they were bigger than me and perhaps more talented than I was, but they never seemed bigger and better than my older brothers seemed in the matches we played in a backyard in Sydney's far west.

When I moved on to grade and representative cricket, and when things got tough, I'd find myself returning to the feeling of joy I had in those backyard matches, and to the simple spirit of competition against my brothers. There is something pure about the idea that past records, statistics and reputation are stripped away in those moments when it is just batter versus bowler. I'd think, *If I found a way to get my brothers out, I'll certainly find a way to get these guys out.*

The morning of day one of a Test match is energising and exciting. You see the crowd start to roll in, the groundsman marking fresh lines in the pitch, the commentators arriving. It's particularly so for a Test match, but even in other forms there's something special about turning up to that fresh grass. Despite playing hundreds of professional games, the scoreboard still starts again at 0–0 and I never know what the game will throw at me. There's a challenge there, and a thrill that today is a fresh opportunity to do something extraordinary.

These moments are my bubbles in the water.

I reckon John Bertrand will always have, deep inside him, that childhood feeling of watching the bubbles go past as he sailed in Port Phillip Bay.

Things can get incredibly complicated when you're doing anything at the highest levels. Questions of politics can intrude, and of ego and money, alongside all of the stresses inherent in being an adult, a dad and a husband. Cricket can become incredibly complicated if you let it. Or you can choose to deal with those complications off the pitch, while on the pitch you play simply, purely and with joy.

I reckon that's the most enjoyable way to play, and it also produces the best results. It also helps me to think about that little boy playing at Mount Riverview, with a pitch mowed out on the lawn, the grass slicked for extra skid, and a trampoline behind me doubling as an electric wickie. I think, *How lucky would he feel to have an opportunity like this?* I reckon, even after my cricket career, it'll be useful sometimes, somehow, to go back to that time and that feeling.

I hope so, anyway.

\*

Before the start of the 2012 London Olympics, Australian hopes and expectations were high, especially in the pool. Our country had a long tradition of excelling in the swimming competition, and the expectation was that Australia's male sprinters would spearhead a successful team.

But it wasn't to be. In race after race, many of the Australian swimmers performed below the viewing public's expectations, and their own. After the final wall touch, the Australian swim team had managed to obtain just one gold medal from a total of ten for the whole Australian Olympic team. It was the worst result for an Australian Olympic swim team in twenty years.

John Bertrand was as involved in those Games as most of us were: as an interested spectator. Since winning the America's Cup, John had lived a life of achievement, but one that had often been out of the limelight. He stayed in competitive sailing, winning three world championships, the most recent less than a decade before 2012, while also excelling in business. As an entrepreneur, he'd built companies in the marine industry and property development, and he had co-founded and launched a digital media company on the Nasdaq exchange in the United States. Of the 2012 Olympics he said, 'I'd just watched it and heard about the Stilnox stuff, that was all.' The 'Stilnox stuff' was the persistent rumour, aired in the media, that some of the swimmers were abusing a drug used to aid sleep and that, perhaps while on the drug, some athletes may have bullied others.

John didn't think too much about the 2012 Olympics when it was over, or the trials and tribulations of Australia's swimmers – until he was contacted in 2013 by Clem Doherty, one the directors of Swimming Australia. Their board had decided to ask the organisation's president, Barclay Nettlefold, to resign in the wake of allegations of improper conduct. The board hoped that John might be Nettlefold's replacement. John told me that initially he didn't have any interest in the job. He didn't know much about swimming – in fact, he'd spent his life trying to stay above the water – and didn't want an admin job. Then he started thinking about the significance of the job and what he could bring to it.

John loves sport and has seen first-hand what it can mean to a country. He loves sailing, but in 2013 he had no illusions about the international sportspeople who were most significant to the Australian public: the national cricket team and the national swimming team. John said he believed that helping either of those programs, if he could, was almost a patriotic obligation. Believing he could help the national swimming program, he agreed to take on the job. 'It was only when I got there that I realised how dysfunctional it all was,' he told me.

John had heard that the organisation had become regrettably political, but he hadn't known to what extent. There were instances of extreme ego, fiefdoms, rivalries and embedded ways of doing things. All of these issues, he believed, were affecting the way the peak body operated, but they also filtered down to the national team, acting as an anchor and impacting performance. A report commissioned by the Swimming Australia board into the issues of the 2012 Olympic team suggested a similar conclusion, speaking of a toxic culture. The report indicated a 'quietly growing lack of focus on people across the board'; this, according to the report, left the competing athletes 'undefended, alone, alienated'. The report confirmed the media reporting of bullying and also the abuse of the drug Stilnox.

Shortly after arriving at the organisation, John wondered if it needed an almost complete reset. He believed that his attitude of over-the-horizon thinking would apply well in this situation, telling all involved that the plan would be to concentrate on radical, long-term future thinking. A business-as-usual attitude would not be accepted.

The move was cheered by the coaches, who felt they now were given licence to break free from the organisational shackles that they believed had been placed upon them and to put everyone else in the organisation on notice. This didn't mean the people working at Swimming Australia were bad at their jobs, it just meant that things were to change quickly, and if anyone found it too hard to move with that change, then they might find it more comfortable to move on.

The Swimming Australia headquarters moved from Canberra to Melbourne, and of the fifty-five permanent staff who had been there when John arrived, only five were still there two years later. Now that the table had been cleared, a new way of doing things had to be established.

John decided that the new Swimming Australia culture might be informed by high-performing teams beyond the sporting arena. Two of the teams that he and the coaches were especially impressed with were the Australian Defence Force's special forces – in particular the full-time commando force, the 2nd Commando Regiment – and the Queensland Ballet.

John and others from Swimming Australia made visits to Holsworthy Barracks, in south-west Sydney, home of the 2nd Commando Regiment and also the Special Forces Training Centre. John said he was amazed by how Australia's Special Operations Command trained its soldiers to prepare for complex environments while dealing with stress at an existential level. He thought there were some lessons that Swimming Australia could take from these soldiers, who had been trained to be in a state of total focus and team unity as they lined up in front of doors where, on the other side, there might be anything, including gunfire.

In the case of the Queensland Ballet, John noticed a different talent that he thought might be useful in a swimming context. He and the Swimming Australia coaches were taken through the dancers' steps by artistic director

Li Cunxin, formerly a principal dancer at the Australian Ballet and the subject of the book and film *Mao's Last Dancer*. With Cunxin's interpretation, John saw ballet dancing in a way he never had before. He was amazed at how often the dancers made mistakes that were imperceptible to nearly anyone watching, and how injuries were accommodated and overcome on stage. The dancers' environment and skills were completely different to those of the commandos: the dancers performed in a largely closed environment, and they were not focused on an end state but rather each step and movement, constantly adapting to be as close as possible to what was planned. John said, 'They had an ability to totally get in their flow and stay in their flow. They make mistakes constantly, but no one ever notices because they are so attuned to their task, they can just adjust and keep going.'

A number of heuristics, methods and goals were developed for the high-performance swimmers, with one North Star sitting above all of this. 'We call it "racing to calmness". It's moving into a world of slow motion. This is the dream. This is what we wanted for our athletes.'

John described exactly what that looks like for a hundred-metre racer. The gun fires and they're off the blocks in 0.5 seconds. The swimmer takes two or three breaths in the first fifty metres, then does a tumble turn and takes two more breaths in the next thirty metres, with the last twenty metres just sprinting. They touch, look up, and see they've smashed the world record. They get out of the pool and say, 'How easy was that,' and add, 'I can't remember the race.'

Performances started to change at the 2016 Rio Olympics, where the Australian team won three gold medals. But it was in Tokyo in 2021 that the most significant dividends were reaped. In the lead-up to the Tokyo Games, another huge cultural shift became embedded in the Olympic team, and that was a change of focus.

One of the most significant findings of the review ordered after the 2012 Games is that there had been an 'increasingly desperate emphasis on gold' – and in the rush to gold, the athletes had felt disconnected from the team and their team-mates. This resulted in many of the swimmers telling the compilers of the report that they felt the London Games were, for them, 'the lonely games'. A decision was made before the Tokyo Games to move the team focus away from gold medals and towards personal bests. In previous Olympics, Swimming Australia set a number of gold medals that would constitute a good meet – that now went out the window. The new key performance indicator was 'conversion rate': the percentage of Australian swimmers who had attained personal bests at the Games. The athletes were no longer told to strive for what the coaches believed would be a gold-medal-winning time; their entire performance focus within the team was now on attaining a personal best.

According to John, 'We went to get rid of winning as a goal, because that wasn't something you could control. You could control your own personal best, so that's what we wanted them to concentrate on.' This, he said, helped to foster team unity, but also helped individual performance, as he believed a concentration on team spirit and away from individual performance would result in better results anyway. 'You already have to be one of the best eight swimmers in your discipline in the world to make the team, so we knew the performances would come.'

There was another cultural change that was explicitly sought for the 2020 Tokyo Games, one designed to foster team unity and also to improve comfort for athletes who were often still teenagers. Regardless of performance, gold-medals conversion rate or any other factor, there would be no judgement. 'Trust was the key,' John said. 'Whether you win or lose, the arms go around you.'

In Tokyo, the Australian swim team won nine golds from a total of twenty-one medals. But better than that, they had a conversion rate of seventy-five per cent, more than twice the rate they had achieved at the 2012 and 2016 Olympics.

\*

There was so much that I identified with when I was talking to John, as a player, leader, athlete and man, but three things were front of mind as we spoke. One was the dynamic between ambition and risk.

I don't think I've ever had the odds stacked so against me as John and his team did when competing in the America's Cup, but as he spoke about that campaign, I did start thinking about the 2023 One Day World Cup in India. Thankfully a lot of the problems John described about the

Australian Olympic swimming team weren't factors for our team, perhaps because we are a little older and more experienced. But when he spoke about the decision-making required to win the America's Cup, I could relate.

In the lead-up to the 2023 World Cup, I felt we had a great side that was playing well – yet if I was being perfectly honest, I thought we weren't good enough to win a tournament in India competing solely on skill. I thought if we performed well, we'd probably be able to finish third or fourth, an outcome that wouldn't be condemned but neither would it really be celebrated. With a result like that, no one would lose their jobs and no fan would walk away from us, but none of us in the teams would remember it especially fondly.

In that moment we had to decide what our ambitions were. If our hope was to perform well and not disappoint anyone, we could have gone on as we had before, but if our ambition was to win the tournament, I thought we had to bring some risk and variance into our decision-making; something that would give us a better chance of winning the competition, but that might see us fail, losing in the round-robin stage or in the early knock-out phase, which would leave us ripe for harsh scrutiny.

We wanted to win, so we decided to embrace that risk. This informed our selection choices and batting order, and it was part of our thinking when we decided to keep Travis Head in the side after he broke his hand in one of the lead-up matches and was not guaranteed to be fit for any of the matches. At another time, in another circumstance, it would have been the right call to send Travis home and replace him with someone else, but it just felt like we couldn't win without his firepower. That was why we picked him and hoped he could play and play well once he recovered.

Travis was integral in the final, smashing a century and grabbing a top-shelf diving catch. Did I know he'd do that and be so important for us? Of course I didn't, but that was our instinct, which was the second thing at the front of my mind as I spoke to John.

When you're an athlete and leader, you so often need to act on instinct, and while I've often relied on it, I've not spent much time thinking about where it comes from.

John said he believes in the Ten Thousand Hours theory of complex mastery, as championed by pop-science writer Malcolm Gladwell. The theory posits that a complex system – be it a musical instrument, the stock market, or a sport – can only be understood by someone after roughly ten thousand hours of interaction with that system. The theory suggests that a sort of unconscious mastery of the system can then emerge. John said that unconscious mastery is often at the heart of instinct, and that makes a lot of sense to me. It suggests that instinct isn't something otherworldly, it's just an unconscious understanding of events born of experience and mental calculation.

This is something that came up again when I interviewed Ronnie Screwvala, the Indian media titan whose creativity changed the Bollywood landscape. So often, over-the-horizon thinking gets you ... well, over the horizon. When you're at the top of your game or at the frontier of your chosen path – whether sport, business or technology – you are crossing into unknown territory. There's some value in looking around at what's worked before, and asking for help from those you respect, but in some respects you're breaking new territory, going on intuition as much as anything, and at the end of the day the call is your own.

There was something else I was thinking about when I was speaking to John: flow state. I don't think you need to have been a high-performance athlete or even an athlete at all in order to understand flow state. We've all been there, totally and fully engaged with the task at hand. If you are an athlete or any type of performer, you've probably spent more time than most other people thinking about how to get into and stay in flow state – through warm-ups, meditation, lucky socks ... whatever works for you.

When talking to John, I wasn't primarily thinking about flow state in the context of my own performance as a player but in the context of other people's performance, in my role as a captain and a leader. When leading a team, you have to consider what conditions your team-mates need for them to have a chance of getting into flow state. You have to foster those conditions if you can, and mediate when team-mates have contradictory needs; for instance, some players like a lot of noise before taking the field, while others want silence.

Above all, though – and this might be one of the most important jobs of a captain, coach or administrator dealing with a high-performance team – you must not be a hindrance on an athlete's ability to get into flow state. I've seen it happen time and time again in my career, and it often happens when the coach or administrator, seeing themselves as integral to success, inserts themselves or team-mates into a situation that didn't need them, thus inviting in the four horsemen of poor performance: stress, anger, clutter and chaos. Even if you don't think you can have a super-positive influence on someone, it's even more important that you avoid being a negative influence on them … and it's amazing how common that is.

The best captains and coaches I've seen get the answer out of the player, rather than telling them what's right or wrong. They almost get the player to self-coach, and respect that the player is experienced enough to diagnose their own problem based on everything they've seen before. Sometimes it's a problem with their technique, sometimes it's tactical, and sometimes it's something else – they're exhausted, they've played too many games in a row, or they've got too much going on in their life. The art is finding and identifying the issue, and then trying to chart out the best path forward for that person.

I thought about flow state when John Bertrand was talking about his time working as the president of Swimming Australia, but even more so when he spoke about his time as a sailor and as the skipper of *Australia II*. More than anything else we spoke about, though, I think I'll remember John talking about how he linked his love of 'watching the bubbles go by' and his performance in the final race of the 1983 America's Cup. I reckon flow state is achieved by doing all the hard work and training, and then, as you perform, taking yourself back to the moment you first fell in love with what you do, performing for performance's sake only.

# 2

## Every inspired person has stood on the shoulders of giants

*A conversation with Richard Scolyer*

IN MAY 2023, PROFESSOR RICHARD SCOLYER WAS ONE of the most notable people in the field of cancer research. As the co-medical director of Melanoma Institute Australia, a not-for-profit organisation and the biggest and best-regarded melanoma research centre of its type in the world, Professor Scolyer – along with his professional partner, Professor Georgina Long, and their incredible team – had led groundbreaking cancer breakthroughs that had significantly changed outcomes and life expectancies for melanoma patients across the world.

Professor Scolyer's career appeared to be at its zenith when, as the co-head of a major institute, he was appearing as the guest speaker at an international conference in Europe. Then his life changed in one of the most radical ways possible.

Professor Scolyer suffered a grand mal seizure, with the cause being an aggressive brain cancer. Shock followed the diagnosis, and disbelief. This type of cancer was a death sentence, because it was essentially incurable.

But what if there was a new treatment? What if some of the research, principles and understanding used by the medical oncologists, surgeons, pathologists and other doctors and researchers at the Melanoma Institute could be applied to Professor Scolyer's brain cancer? Could they save his life? By his own estimation, almost certainly not. Could they lengthen his life? Possibly. Could they gain an incredible amount of data and potentially usher in new treatments that might lengthen the lives of thousands and perhaps even help discover a cure? They might.

Yet if they were to do this, they'd have to do it very quickly – and also bravely, as all involved would be charging into unknown territory. At every step, the possibility of the treatment shortening, worsening or perhaps ending Professor Scolyer's life was there.

So how did they move forward then, and how do they keep moving forward today? How does Richard Scolyer keep working and keep living, with such a cold shadow at his back? It seems there's only one way, and that's with an immense sense of purpose.

*

My mum, Maria Cummins, was diagnosed with breast cancer when I was in high school. At that time I assumed her cancer would be like any other illness I'd had or observed, coming and going like a flu or a stomach bug. I thought she would be sick while undergoing treatment for about six months, but then after that it would all be gone and I would never need to worry about it again. And after the treatment, for the best part of ten years, that was what happened. What I and my siblings hadn't fully grasped yet was that she would never be totally rid of cancer, and she and Dad both knew that it would one day return.

For more than a decade and a half, my mum was a mother like any other – better than most, I reckon – but she was also a patient, all through my teenage life and beyond. Her cancer persisted, sometimes active, sometimes dormant, and for the last eight years or so of her life it was also ever-present in ours. Diagnosis, treatment, remission, diagnosis and then more treatment became an embedded part of our family life. There was school and sport and friends and family; birthdays, Christmases, holidays and exams – and there was also cancer.

I talked to Rich about Mum, about how she felt and about how the cancer never truly went away. It always ticked away in the back of your mind. You always worried, and that worry came in a cycle – gaining in intensity in the lead-up to the next scan, relief at no signs of recurrence, and then a slowly building dread in the years leading to the next scan.

For the most part, Mum didn't want to make a fuss. She didn't want us kids burdened with the situation. So she would always crack on, speak about the positives, say things like, 'Who cares? It's only hair,' after her chemo treatments. I think she didn't want the fact that she had cancer to define her. Deep down, she probably knew what was going on but in some ways didn't want to accept it.

Eventually things changed, and Mum managed to come to terms with it through communication. She didn't hide anything from us kids. Nothing was sugar-coated, nothing was ignored. Nothing was minimised, and no question was off limits. We didn't pretend it wasn't happening, nor did we let the cancer stop us from living our lives and being a family.

Cancer being what it is, though, it was always there, like a smell you can't get out of the upholstery in your car. You can concentrate on something else and perhaps even forget about it for a while, but it's always there, lingering.

I was reminded of that when I met Richard ('Please, call me Rich') Scolyer, his wife, Dr Katie Nicoll, and their teenage son, Matt, at their inner-west home. After introductions we sat at the kitchen table, where we chatted about cricket (which Matt's a big fan of) and exercise (which Rich does a lot of) and the weather, as we shared chips and cake. Then it was time to talk about cancer.

Rich told me a cancer story that was mind-blowing and exceptional in parts, and commonplace and familiar in others. His experience as a husband and dad who's battling against cancer is similar to that of so many Australians. At the time Rich was diagnosed, he was one of more than 400 Australians diagnosed with a cancer that day, and one of more than 165,000 Australians diagnosed that year. Rich is now part of the forty per cent of the Australian public who will be diagnosed with cancer in their lifetime, which means if you don't get cancer at some point, you will almost certainly be in the position I was in, as the loved one of someone who has it.

Those statistics are the depressing part of the Australian cancer picture, but there's an uplifting part also: the drastic improvement in cancer outcomes during the past few decades. Cancer remissions and survival rates have skyrocketed, and this is where the mind-blowing and exceptional part of Rich Scolyer's story begins.

Every cancer researcher puts greatly needed runs on the board, but only a few get to hit the winning runs that are a research breakthrough or a deployable treatment. Rich has not only hit those winning runs once, but he may also again be in a partnership that does it twice. And the second time, one of the lives he might be extending could be his own.

\*

Rich told me he links his drive towards medical research all the way back to 1970, when he was just a little boy and a medical mystery befell his mum, Jenny Scolyer. He was four when it happened. Jenny, a teacher like my mum, had a series of turns later recognised as strokes. They left her unable to speak or move much.

It's a time Rich vividly remembers. He remembers his mother being bed-bound in their Launceston home. He remembers his mother and father travelling to Melbourne for medical treatment. He remembers being shipped off into the Tasmanian countryside, where he could be cared for by an aunt and uncle, while his older brother was cared for by a different aunt and uncle who lived near his school.

Richard said his family – including his aunt and uncle – were caring and loving, and did the best they could. Yet he also said he'd never forget the isolation and confusion of that period. That's what he remembers most vividly, Rich said: not facts or circumstances, but feelings. 'It was a very hard time. I still get quite emotional when I speak about it. I had serious concerns about what may happen to us.'

Doctors eventually identified why Jenny Scolyer had suffered these strokes. Rich's mum was taking a contraceptive pill, then an emerging treatment, that had very high levels of the hormone oestrogen. That hormone had helped create blood clots in her body that had travelled into her brain, where they had cut off the blood and therefore the oxygen to essential brain tissue. Jenny was young when this happened, and thanks to neuroplastic effects that allow the brain to regain function after brain damage, she fully recovered her movement and speech functions. But Rich never fully recovered. He told me that even now that period of his life lives with him.

The idea that microscopic changes in the body can result in monumental changes in a life and a family stayed with Rich. So did the idea that advances in treatments could be the difference between happiness and sadness, and even life and death.

After finishing high school in Launceston, Rich enrolled at the University of Tasmania. He graduated first with a Bachelor of Medical Science, then a Bachelor of Medicine and a Bachelor of Surgery, without knowing exactly what kind of medical career he'd like to have. He was twenty-four, and the one thing he knew for sure was that he wanted to get out of Tasmania for a bit, so he went to Adelaide, where he worked at the Royal Adelaide Hospital as a resident medical officer. After a couple of years working in Gosford and the United Kingdom and travelling overseas, he decided to study pathology, the branch of medicine that concentrates on the study and diagnosis of illness. He moved to Canberra, where he worked for a year as a haematology registrar, concentrating on blood, and then for the next few years in tissue pathology. Needing to work in at least one other hospital to finish his specialist training as a registrar, he moved to Sydney so he could work at Royal Prince Alfred Hospital, south-west of the CBD.

This decision was to prove fateful in two ways. At RPA, Rich fell in love with another young doctor specialising in pathology: Katie Nicoll, now his wife. He also eventually narrowed the focus of his specialisation to cancer diagnosis and research, particularly in melanoma.

After Rich finished as a registrar in 2001, the hospital offered him a full-time job that was broken up into two halves. In one half of the job, he worked as a staff histopathology specialist, which entailed diagnosing and categorising cancers as patients presented. In the other half, he worked as a researcher in a specialised unit that was looking to improve the treatment of melanoma, a type of skin cancer.

Melanoma disproportionately affects Australians. It's a cancer that often develops as the result of UV radiation exposure, which due to the position of the sun, our lifestyle and the lack of pollution in our cities, Australians are heavily exposed to. In fact, Australia has the highest rate of melanoma and other skin cancers in the world, at nearly ten times the global average, despite massive public education efforts.

The opportunity to work on melanoma research at Royal Prince Alfred Hospital was an exciting prospect for a young pathologist like Rich. With more melanoma patients coming through the doors of RPA than perhaps any other hospital in the world, it's a place where a great deal of data can be analysed and a strong impact from treatment breakthroughs can be felt.

Rich said that this specialised unit – then known as the Sydney Melanoma Unit and now Melanoma Institute Australia – 'provided me with an incredible chance to contribute'. And contribute he did. While he was working at the unit, melanoma treatment underwent a seismic shift, and he was a big part of that.

When Rich started at the Institute, treatment for melanoma was mostly limited to surgery, and there was no effective treatment for patients who had advanced melanoma. 'At that time there weren't any drugs that worked for melanoma,' he told me. 'Getting the diagnosis right and getting patients the right treatment and the right surgery was really important, but when it had spread around your body, basically most people were potentially in serious trouble.' Even just over ten years ago, if you were a melanoma patient and your cancer had started to spread distantly in your body, you were likely to be dead within a year. Breakthroughs, according to Rich, were tantalisingly close but not yet ready for clinical trials, the essential last step for a widespread rollout to patients.

Working under and mentored by famed cancer clinicians and researchers Professor John Thompson and Professor Stan McCarthy, Rich helped develop a culture of working effectively and cohesively as a multidisciplinary and complementarily skilled team at Melanoma Institute that fostered advances in treatments, trials and, finally, common use for melanoma patients in Australia and overseas. It's a culture that many leaders of many teams, including mine, could learn from. Rich said that in fact some of the most important factors contributing to the scientific research leaps occurred because of this culture.

The two professors Rich worked under came from very different fields. The late Professor McCarthy was a pathologist like Rich, meaning he spent much of his time looking down a microscope, considering biopsies of human tissues. Professor Thompson, who has since retired, was a surgeon; he worked with patients to figure out where and when to remove cancers and how best to provide for their ongoing management. Both roles are essential to understanding melanoma, but each man held just once piece of a very large puzzle. Other medical researchers and doctors with different expertise – medical oncologists, surgical oncologists, pathologists, radiation oncologists, dermatologists, radiologists and others – have held pieces of that puzzle too.

According to Rich, the Institute is a centre of excellence primarily because it has been able to apply its findings to points of strategic focus. Its culture allows radical thought and individual brilliance, Rich said, but always in a way that's subservient to that strategic focus. This hasn't happened within a strict, hierarchical information structure, with junior researchers and doctors feeding specialised information to more senior staff, who feed information to department heads, who eventually feed information to Rich and his co-medical director, who synthesise all of it and send orders back down the chain. Instead, it has happened through a flat, communal structure that has encouraged pathologists to ask questions about surgery, surgeons about medical oncology, medical oncologists about psychology and so on, all in the presence of leaders like Rich, who then establish, focus and set agendas.

Rich told me that one of the most significant ways the Institute has fostered its culture is through a weekly multidisciplinary team meeting (or MDT meeting). 'It's at that meeting that a lot of our research questions come up – questions we need to address to go forward,' he said. During an MDT meeting, all attendees are invited to talk about current unresolved melanoma cases at their clinics or the hospital, and how these cases relate to current and potentially future treatment. Often more than sixty healthcare professionals and researchers attend the meetings, where they invite other doctors, healthcare professionals and researchers to suggest possible resolutions to problems that they haven't been able to address alone. Rich said the meetings have always been patient-focused and in the service of curing or treating current melanomas. He added that MDT meetings have also ended up being one of the Institute's most important research tools and a major influence on their strategic work. 'We went from strength to strength,' he explained. 'Critical questions we needed to answer were starting to be answered by research and clinical trials, and we did some things that have started to make a difference to how patients are managed.'

Since 2017, when Rich and medical oncologist Professor Georgina Long became co-medical directors of the Institute, they have taken turns chairing the MDT meetings. Rich told me he and Georgina were 'standing on the shoulders of giants' when they took on the role of co-medical directors, while humbly accepting that some of the most incredible breakthroughs have happened since then.

When he and Professor Long took over in 2017, there were some drug treatments for advanced melanoma available on the Pharmaceutical Benefits Scheme due to the work of Professor Long and the medical oncology team at the Institute, along with colleagues from around the world. A public education prevention campaign and surgical improvements meant there had been improvements in patient management, but none that were drastic yet. Rich and Professor Long were confident those outcomes were coming, though. Shortly after becoming co-medical directors, they announced a pledge that there should be no more melanoma deaths in Australia by the year 2030. Now we're about halfway from the pledge's announcement date to 2030, and outcomes for melanoma patients have become significantly better. As recently as 2010, the five-year survival rate for a patient with an advanced melanoma was about five per cent, meaning that if twenty patients had an advanced melanoma, it was expected that nineteen of them would be dead half a decade later. Today the long-term survival rate is fifty-five per cent.

This is in no small part due to the drug therapies that Rich, Professor Long and others at the Institute have helped to conceive, develop, test or roll out, many of which are government-approved and funded treatments. One has proven to be particularly effective and has been described as a potential game-changer across the board. While it was first used only for melanoma, it's now used for a range of cancers, and the hope is that it might be effectively deployed against the highly aggressive brain cancer that Rich now suffers from.

\*

Since I started playing cricket in the nineties, perceptions about sun safety have changed. Bare arms and heads have given way to long sleeves and brims, and the application and reapplication of sunscreen has become as normal as hydration and rehydration. This change has been primarily due to people gaining a better understanding of what's required to avoid skin cancer, which is generally more preventable than most other cancers. Minimising excessive UV exposure with sunscreen works well; hats and covering clothes work even better. As professional cricketers who follow the summer sun around the world we know that if you are going to be out in the middle of the pitch in the sun all day, you need to take it seriously.

When a melanoma first develops, the best way to minimise harm is to identify the cancer before it spreads and becomes an advanced melanoma. For those of us with Cricket Australia contracts, this is something that's done with the help of the association, which holds education sessions about what kinds of marks, moles and lesions we should get checked out. It also facilitates annual skin checks for players and former players. It's super common for those former players, especially the older ones, to have melanomas cut out of them, after childhoods and careers spent in the sun with little protection.

For those of you who don't have a Cricket Australia contract, skin cancer checks can be done easily pretty much everywhere in Australia by booking an appointment at the Cancer Council website. Yet despite being sun safe and despite conducting rigorous skin checks, some Australians will still develop melanomas that require surgery and other treatment.

Once a melanoma has been identified, the depth of the tumour is a significant factor in its treatment and outcome. For melanomas that haven't spread beyond the epidermis and dermis of the skin, safe and simple surgery is the best option. This surgery will usually be the end of that melanoma. When the melanoma has spread beyond the skin into the subcutaneous tissue, surgery will probably not be the end of that melanoma.

These often become advanced melanomas that spread around the body, and they used to be all but a death sentence. But not anymore. Drug treatments, many pioneered by Melanoma Institute, allow some patients to live full and happy lives and, in some instances, find themselves cleared of cancer.

The most significant and effective of those treatments is immunotherapy, which is designed to amplify the body's natural immune response to cancer, attacking the disease at a cellular level. I asked Rich about immunotherapy, and what was so significant about its discovery in combating cancers. As he told me, immunotherapy is designed to emulate and enhance processes that happen in the body every day, to ensure that cancers don't develop or are destroyed when they do. 'We all develop cancers,' said Rich. 'I don't know if it's every day, but it's frequent ... especially in older patients, and your body's immune system finds them and kills them off before you know you had cancer. Some cancers become clinically evident because they can hide themselves from the immune system and grow.'

He explained that the way cancers hide themselves is by using a sort of molecular camouflage, wrapping themselves up in a way that the immune system doesn't recognise as cancer. One of the most significant advances in cancer therapy was when researchers found treatments that strip away this molecular camouflage, allowing the body to attack the cancer cells, which it can do incredibly effectively.

Another advancement was the development of drugs that supercharge the natural processes that attack cancer cells.

Immunotherapies are now widespread treatments for a number of cancers, but it all started with melanoma because, as Rich told me, the characteristics of melanoma lend themselves to immunotherapy.

One such characteristic is a byproduct of how melanomas develop. They are formed due to mutations in the skin's DNA, which create chemicals that can tell the body to activate its immune response. A feature of immunotherapy is the use of drugs to break down the barriers the tumour puts up against the immune system to supercharge and facilitate this response. The identification and manipulation of this process was one of the breakthroughs that the Institute contributed to. It has led to the immense success of immunotherapy.

Another breakthrough they contributed to was the realisation that immunotherapy is far more effective when it's deployed as quickly as possible, before any other treatments – including surgery, radiation and chemotherapy. 'When there's more cancer, the immunotherapy often works better, basically,' Rich said, adding that the shock and side effects of other treatments, particularly chemotherapy, can also affect immunotherapy.

These days, most patients presenting with melanomas that have spread locally or are advanced are treated with immunotherapy early on. This has resulted in many cancers shrinking or staying static; in some instances, other treatments haven't been necessary, with the cancer all but disappearing. Since becoming a treatment for melanoma, immunotherapy has also become a common treatment for head and neck, bladder, kidney, liver and lung cancers, as well as leukaemia and lymphoma.

There is also one person in the world being treated with pre-surgery (neoadjuvant) combination immunotherapy for glioblastoma, the most aggressive and lethal brain cancer known. That person is Rich Scolyer.

\*

In May 2023, the Spanish island of Ibiza hosted the World Triathlon Multisport Championships, which included the World Aquathlon Championships: essentially a short-course triathlon without the bike leg. This competition was to be undertaken on a quiet beach in the town of Santa Eulalia, known as a family destination and as a getaway from the nightclubs and parties that Ibiza is so famous for.

It was an appropriate venue for Rich Scolyer to compete in the World Aquathlon Championships alongside his teenage daughter, Emily, and Professor Georgina Long. The trip was Emily's idea. While Rich had his eyes on a different international triathlon competition later in the year, this event worked for both their schedules – Emily was on a break from her university studies, and Rich and Professor Long were scheduled to be in Europe to speak at a conference – so he relented. All three of them performed well, and Rich finished in the top twenty of his age category.

Afterwards, he said goodbye to Emily and flew home. Two weeks later, he flew to Kraków, Poland, with Katie.

There he presented a talk in front of an international audience of mostly pathologists about his experience, and the research Melanoma Institute was pioneering. Neither in Ibiza nor in Kraków was there any indication that something was seriously wrong with Rich's brain.

After heading to a mountain resort on Poland's southern border for a planned trek, Rich started to feel a bit off. The day after the trek, he felt a little nauseous and dizzy. He attributed the feeling to fatigue, altitude and his consumption of Polish lager. Later that day, Rich lay on the floor and suffered a grand mal seizure. He and Katie went to a local hospital for a CT scan of his brain, which would look for a haemorrhage, a common cause of such a seizure. No haemorrhage was found.

Normally an Australian in Poland would have had to wait to get home before they could have a more comprehensive brain scan, but the organisers of the conference arranged for Rich to be taken to Kraków, where he could immediately get an MRI. That scan found something in his brain, but the Polish physicians could not make a definitive diagnosis just on the scan. The abnormality looked like a tumour, but they could not exclude a herpes virus infection.

Rich and Katie looked at the scan and Katie sent it to Professor Long, who consulted specialist colleagues in Sydney and elsewhere. They all came to the same chilling realisation: the lesion was almost certainly a glioblastoma, a very aggressive and almost always fatal brain cancer.

'My first thought was, *I'm not getting out of this*,' said Rich. 'It's devastating to think you're not going to be able to lead your normal life that you've enjoyed so much when you still have so much life you want to lead.'

While Rich and Katie were reeling from the news, Professor Long started thinking about how some of the treatments pioneered for melanoma might be applied to the cancer in her colleague's brain. Key in her thoughts was the possibility of using some of the new immunotherapy protocols that worked so well in advanced melanoma, but were not yet standard or proven.

Combination immunotherapy given before surgery had never been attempted on a glioblastoma, in part because of how quickly treatment must be applied to such a cancer and how traditional glioblastoma treatment suppresses the immune system. By the time a glioblastoma is discovered, the patient is often in immediate mortal danger due to the pressure the tumor exerts on the brain. After it's suspected that a patient has developed a glioblastoma, a biopsy is usually undertaken to confirm the diagnosis. Then the patient might be given a course of steroids to lessen the swelling in their brain, and a surgery known as debulking is imminently scheduled to take away as much cancer as possible, while trying to minimise brain functional deficits. After the debulking, radiotherapy and chemotherapy are usually given and the patient essentially waits for the cancer to recur. When that happens, the patient is usually in the last months of their life; after recurrence a patient may not be able to undertake a second debulking operation, as glioblastoma often returns aggressively, meaning that too much of the brain would need to be removed.

After the glioblastoma was discovered, scans showed that Rich's brain wasn't suffering the pressure effects patients often experience when diagnosed. He believes this may have been due to him experiencing natural swelling at a high altitude – in a slightly swollen brain, the glioblastoma triggered the seizure ahead of when it would have done so at sea level.

Rich wanted to return to Sydney before commencing treatment, so with some anti-seizure medicine in his blood, as well as trust that in the pressurised cabin the cancer wouldn't press against his brain and cause another seizure, he and Katie flew home.

By the time they arrived, Professor Long and other doctors and scientists at the Institute had spent three days discussing the specifics of Rich's prognosis. They presented him with a potential treatment plan, including experimental treatments such as pre-surgery combination immunotherapy, which was a relatively safe treatment for melanoma but presented unique risks in Rich's case.

Rich was advised by the team that there were potential risks that immunotherapy could cause damage to his other organs, and delaying the debulking surgery could allow the glioblastoma to keep growing insidiously through his brain, potentially with grave results. Some doctors argued that there was no point in taking on all this risk that would likely garner no reward, as they believed that the blood–brain barrier – a semipermeable membrane that separates the brain from the rest of the vascular system – wouldn't allow the immunotherapy drugs to enter the brain. But to Rich, with the expertise of Professor Long in his corner, the decision to try this treatment was a 'no-brainer'. He wanted to live, and not just the handful of months that would be expected from a normal treatment path. Professor Long had devised and led the first trial of immunotherapy in melanoma that had spread to the brain, and it had shown that the drugs were effective in getting immune cells targeting the cancer cells to cross the blood–brain barrier. 'We had, I guess, an informed hunch,' Rich told me.

To me, Rich's act was incredibly selfless. Sure he had a desire to live longer than a normal treatment path might have allowed him, but he was willing to put himself further out there just to make a difference. What are the chances that someone in his role would also be placed in the rare position of being able to make a difference – and then choose to do so?

After Rich decided to attempt Professor Long's combination immunotherapy plan, the most immediate concern for him and the team was figuring out how long to hold off before they debulked the tumour. Rich and Professor Long discussed the plan with a trusted surgeon, Associate Professor Brindha Shivalingam, who had worked with them for more than a decade at the Institute. They were asking her, after a biopsy to confirm the diagnosis, to hold off on the crucial debulking surgery until Rich could receive as much immunotherapy as possible. 'She was very supportive to go down this path, but a little nervous,' Rich told me. 'Then we talked about how long we could leave between the two procedures, and we wanted six weeks. She said, "Oh, no way!"'

The debulking of a glioblastoma is always a tricky surgery, as the cancer spreads tentacles through the brain. A neurosurgeon always wants to cut out as much cancer as possible, but has to balance this with concerns about taking away healthy tissue used for cognition, memory and, indeed, life itself. Rich's surgery would be especially tricky because he was asking for it to be delayed, potentially giving the tentacles time to spread further.

Associate Professor Shivalingam said that after six weeks there was a significant chance the tumour would have spread so extensively that surgery would be impossible, or that Rich could be left severely impacted. In her opinion, it had to happen as quickly as possible after the biopsy – but if there was any chance the immunotherapy would work, time was needed. Eventually Associate Professor Shivalingam, Rich and Professor Long agreed that Rich would undertake the initial open biopsy in three days' time and the debulking surgery sixteen days after that.

Rich had one other request of Associate Professor Shivalingam. For his biopsy he wanted to have a craniotomy, meaning part of his skull would be removed, instead of a minimally invasive needle core biopsy. This procedure would mean there was more risk, something surgeons are reluctant to take on, but it would also mean they could collect more tissue and therefore generate more research data. This wouldn't help Rich but could be uniquely useful to researchers and potentially other brain-cancer patients in the future. Associate Professor Shivalingam agreed immediately. She was trying to save Rich's life while also helping to bring in a new treatment for a deadly cancer.

In May 2023, Rich Scolyer successfully undertook his open biopsy. Then, sixteen days later, after he had received combination immunotherapy, he prepared for his second craniotomy. He also prepared for a very uncertain future. Brain surgeons are some of the smartest people in the world, yet brain surgery is still an imperfect science; all kinds of issues may arise, including significant cognitive and emotional changes. Dr Shivalingam would have to take healthy brain tissue along with the tumour, so Rich didn't know exactly who he would be when he woke up.

He went under the knife, then came back up again. The debulking surgery was a success, removing much of the cancer without any major complications. Furthermore, Rich was still the bloke he'd been before the surgery. Now the question of whether the immunotherapy was actually doing anything hung over him.

Pathologists and researchers compared tissue from the initial open biopsy with tissue removed during the debulking to see what, if any, change could be detected. Only thirteen days after the start of immunotherapy, absence of evidence wasn't evidence of absence, but Rich desperately hoped for some indication in the tissue collected in the second surgery that the immunotherapy was doing something.

'In what we saw, we were blown away,' Rich told me. 'We couldn't believe it.'

The second tissue samples showed three things. Firstly, in the initial biopsy, the doctors and researchers had found that there weren't very many lymphocytes (immune cells) in Rich's tumour; now, thirteen days later, there were ten times as many. Secondly, the types of immune cells in the tumour had changed; in the second tissue samples, they found activated lymphocytes, meaning these lymphocytes were actively fighting against the tumour. Thirdly, they found that a drug used in the therapy was bound to the activated lymphocytes, meaning the blood–brain barrier had undoubtedly been crossed. 'I couldn't believe it – that means the drugs are having an effect,' said Rich. 'Whether they result in better outcomes, we don't know, but [those results] mean it's worth exploring.'

\*

For Rich's type of glioblastoma, the average time of recurrence – or the time it takes for the cancer to return after debulking – is six months. I met with Rich eight months after his diagnosis, and when I did there was no indication of recurrence. The experimental therapies were not yet causing catastrophic effects, either. There were some side effects, including abnormal liver function tests, also lethargy and a low haemoglobin level that was concerning – until the doctors realised that these effects were due to the sheer volume of blood that Rich was giving in the service of research.

As I write, more than four months after our meeting, an MRI recently confirmed that Rich still has no sign of cancer recurrence, and Professor Long and the team are planning for a clinical trial with the treatment. It's been more than a year since Rich's diagnosis, and there are indications – in his pathology and in the time he's spent without a recurrence – that the experimental treatments may be doing something good. Exactly how effective they are is not known, so Rich is cherishing his time, which is not to say that he's drastically changed his life. He told me he's always valued time with his family, and that won't change. When I spoke to him, he had just finished a sixteen-kilometre run, and he said that he hopes the amount of exercise he does won't change either, as it's essential for his physical and mental health. That pretty much just leaves work, which he still does too.

The nature of that work has changed, however. Rich has decided that to make the greatest impact on outcomes, he should step back from some of his diagnostic duties at the Royal Prince Alfred Hospital and work more in management, research and as an ambassador, raising awareness of sun safety and early melanoma detection, as well as raising funds, private and public, for the Institute and other cancer research centres. This ambassadorial work was supercharged on Australia Day 2024, when Rich and Professor Long were announced as the Australians of the Year. The honour recognised their enduring partnership and the Institute's incredible research success – past, present and, hopefully, future.

Some people may have chosen to step away from work completely and concentrate on their own welfare when given a diagnosis like Rich's, but he told me that cancer research has been his life's project and that it wouldn't feel right to walk away when he can contribute so much.

Rich said that the work of Melanoma Institute wouldn't have been possible without contributions from patients, which he has found exceptional and inspiring. An example of one such contribution is a trove of tissue collected from consenting former patients dating back to the 1990s, in storage at the Institute and known as the biospecimen bank. 'It's a resource like no other. The tumour tissue gives us these opportunities to do incredible research, which has changed the field,' said Rich. 'I think it's amazing. It has something to do with the Australian ethos [and a] culture of generosity.' Much of the tissue has come from patients who weren't cured of their melanoma but were able to leave a legacy and, ultimately, contribute to humanity.

Rich told me that he often thinks about his legacy. He thinks about it as a friend, father, husband and patient – saying that this thought pushed him to write a memoir and join social media platforms – but also a scientist and member of the human race, which are the things that keep him working. No one person is going to cure cancer, but some people are in a position to contribute more than most to the cause. Rich is one of those people, and he told me that this does give him comfort on the darkest nights he has experienced since Poland.

'Sometimes it feels like I'm in an incredibly exciting time,' said Rich. 'It actually feels great to be able to contribute and to try to help others. While my cancer journey is still young and the path ahead is uncertain, I feel lucky and very grateful for the opportunities provided. I am also thankful for the insights and acumen of my friend and colleague Professor Georgina Long and the fantastic team of clinicians and researchers for all they have done for me.'

I asked Rich if he was ever tempted to stop. After a diagnosis like that, some people might shut down and isolate themselves from the world, while others might want to see as much of it as they could. Rich told me he thought about it for a week, but realised he would have got bored of that. His kids were in school and he didn't want to disrupt his family's life, but he also didn't want to sit around twiddling his thumbs either. So he went back to work.

*

My mum passed away in March 2023. Her passing was devastating and shocking, personally seismic, but a commonplace occurrence also. We all experience loss, and often people are lost too young. There are few things more awful than losing a loved one. The pain is immense and enduring, but after the pain is folded into you, it feels as though some of the secrets of life are revealed. Or, at the very least, some of life's priorities. Since Mum's passing, I worry less about the highs and lows of cricket and being a public person.

When I was first selected in the Test team, I worried quite a lot about how I might perform. But Mum told me not to worry about it, because even if it was a total calamity, I'd have a baggy green and I would have been out on the pitch playing for Australia. It was more than I could ever have hoped for as a kid – and besides, even if I did play as badly as anyone could, I'd still come back to a home in which people loved me. Then it was Mum, Dad and my siblings; now it's Becky and Albie.

I still take Mum's words on board when things are tough on the pitch. I remind myself how awesome it is that I'm playing for Australia, or an Indian Premier League team or whatever, and regardless of how I play, I still get to go home to a family who love me.

Mum also taught me a lot about what living a good life can mean. For her, life was about spending time with the people you love, helping out those in the community who need it, and trying to find joy and adventure in everything you do. That's how Mum lived her life, and I think Rich sees the world through a similar lens.

After a recurrence of Mum's cancer, Dad suggested to her that she might want to retire from teaching, but similar to Rich, she said that was the last thing she wanted to do. She loved teaching. She loved the students and how they progressed; she loved being able to give back to this life and our community. Mum found purpose and passion in her work much as Rich does, and she kept working as long as she could.

I thought of my mum often when speaking to Rich, and it made me reflect on the importance of where you allocate your time. Hopefully I've got a long time left in life, but even then it is finite. It made me wonder, where might I want to spend each hour of what time I have remaining? And what are the few priorities that are most important to me? In cricket, the conventional wisdom is that if you are playing all forms of the game, with a schedule that covers every month of the year in an endless summer, you play every game you can. Perhaps there is a better way. I don't think you can ever get it exactly right, but Rich's story enforced to me the importance of not walking through life on autopilot, and questioning the conventional wisdom. Now I try to be deliberate with how I spend my time – not just with the things I'm passionate about but also with the people who matter. It also occurred to me that if you can get the kind of news Rich was given in May 2023, or the news Mum was given a few years previously, and you still want to do the work you were doing before, then you probably have already seen deeper into life than most.

# 3

## Beyond all of the noise and glory of leadership is the work, which can be a harbour when you need one

*A conversation with Julia Gillard*

I was a bit nervous about meeting Julia Gillard. I'd still been in high school when she was prime minister of Australia, and I wasn't exactly reading the papers every day. What I did know about her was that she's a little bit private.

In the years since, I've met half a dozen Australian prime ministers – as the Australian cricket team gets invited to Kirribilli House every year on New Year's Day – and some others overseas leaders as well, and the first thing I always think about is how much power rests on one person's shoulders. The second thing I wonder is how they function with so much responsibility in so many areas. How do they manage that from a performance optimisation perspective? Where do they find the space to think, or just be themselves?

It's always blown me away how many different roles there are that a prime minister takes on. There's the executive side, making decisions and policy. There's the public-facing side, making speeches and consulting with the community.

There's international relations. And, sometimes, there is a symbolic aspect to leadership too.

As captain, a lot of the decision-making of my role is done within and around the team, in selection, and in conversation with coaches, administrators and my fellow players – and, of course, also on the pitch, where I need to make tactical decisions and try to lead by example.

There's also that public-facing role – the work that I do in front of a camera and microphone, or live before an audience, where I can explain my decisions and thoughts, and where they will be tested and questioned.

As representatives of our nation, there is of course an international relations aspect to being a cricketer.

And then there's the final role: the influence that leaders wield simply by virtue of their station. This goes beyond decisions that relate to winning and losing, and beyond putting on a public face – it's about leading by example, and being the kind of person I want to see more of.

There are so many different aspects that are all vital for success. Some days I just want to get out on the pitch and play, but I know there are other important responsibilities to the role, like attending press conferences or dealing with commercial arrangements. Doing the work on the pitch is obviously crucial, but if you can't explain and articulate that work, then you'll fail to bring others along with you. If you have a well-explained plan but can't execute it, you're a dreamer, not a leader. If you are a good operator and a good communicator but don't stand for anything, don't inspire anyone and win only for your own benefit, you've also failed as a leader.

This brings me to former Prime Minister Julia Gillard, who, as Australia's first female prime minister, acquired a more powerfully symbolic role than any other Australian in the top job. In the 2010 federal election Julia was installed as an elected prime minister but in charge of a minority Labor government that relied on the support of the Greens member and three independents. While minority governments are not unknown in Australian politics, they are unusual, and it was easy for political opponents and the media to characterise the arrangement as unstable. Yet, despite all of this, lead Julia did.

Through internal criticism and leaks, as well as bitter personal and gendered assaults, Australia's first female prime minister led a minority government that executed policy and changed the country. She did this in public, inspiring Australians (especially women and girls); she did it at her desk, where she seems to have been particularly comfortable; and she did it by knowing exactly what she wanted her government to achieve and how to get it done.

\*

During her political career, Julia Gillard sometimes participated in events at primary schools, where it was common for little girls to approach her and tell her that they wanted to become prime minister one day.

'I wonder where that comes from,' Julia said to me. 'Because I was never like that.' She added that she 'didn't grow up in the kind of family or indeed in the kind of era where a child, particularly a young girl, would form a view that they were going to be a leader in any kind of "capital L" sense.'

Julia was born in Wales and migrated to Australia with her parents at age four. Her mother worked as a cook in an aged-care facility, and her father trained and then worked as a psychiatric nurse. She didn't grow up as someone who would expect to lead anything really, let alone the country. 'Primary school, high school, I was never a sporty kid, so the kind of leadership opportunities that come with doing what you do ... that was never me,' she said. She might not have been a good athlete, but she was a good and conscientious student. At Unley High, a state school in Adelaide's south, she was made prefect in 'some kind of faux election ... from the people the teachers had decided were suitable'. She added, 'That's kind of the entry point [into leadership] for me.'

After graduating from school and starting undergraduate degrees at the University of Adelaide, Julia became interested in and concerned about proposed education cutbacks, joining the student union and then becoming its leader. She was the first student to lead the Adelaide University Union, and she eventually became the vice-president and then the second female president of the Australian Union of Students, a national body. Julia told me that in these leadership roles, 'You would have people saying to you that, given you are interested in public policy and leadership, you should think about running for Parliament.'

In 1986, Julia graduated with Bachelor of Arts and Bachelor of Laws degrees. She then worked as an industrial relations lawyer at the law firm Slater and Gordon. Having worked heavily in unionism, education and industrial relations, Julia thought she could contribute positively to federal policy in each of those areas, so she made an attempt to enter federal Parliament. She said, 'It took me more than a decade from the time I decided I'd like to do it to ending up getting an opportunity to do it.'

After attempts at multiple lower-house preselections and one tilt at the Senate, Julia was finally elected to federal Parliament in 1998. She was thirty-seven.

'If you asked me when I got in on the first day in Parliament [what my ideal career would be], I would have said, "If I get to be a minister in a Labor government, if I get to be Minister for Education or maybe Minster for Industrial Relations" – that was my legal specialty – "if I get to do that, that would be the ultimate."' But for some years that goal was unattainable, as John Howard's Coalition government had a strong electoral grasp on power. Julia said, 'One of the fascinations and one of the frustrations of politics is that it's not an effort-in, outcome-out kind of pursuit. There's all sorts of random, unpredictable factors. Part of it is the merit of you and your team, and it's also whether the times suit your brand of politics.'

There are opportunities in opposition, however. Julia became known as an excellent communicator and, in political circles, was well regarded as someone who could understand the minutiae of policy.

In 2001, Labor suffered another electoral defeat, with the Coalition winning eighty-two seats and Labor winning only sixty-five. Julia became shadow minister in a number of portfolios. Then, in 2004, John Howard's government won an election that most believed Labor was going to win – instead, Labor lost even more seats than they had in 2001. Julia started to be mentioned as a potential future leader or deputy leader, openly by the media and quietly by her colleagues.

The Labor Party was suffering a personality crisis, best exemplified by its decision to elevate Mark Latham to its leadership in 2003. After he vacated that position in 2005, stalwart Kim Beazley became interim leader of the party, but many Labor MPs believed new blood was sorely needed at the top. This came in the form of Kevin Rudd and Julia Gillard, rising stars within the party who worked hard and polled very well. The pair became leaders of the Labor Party in December 2006 and then of the country in 2007.

Labor won in a landslide that even saw John Howard lose his own seat. When Labor was sworn in to government, Julia Gillard became Australia's first female deputy prime minister. She was also the Minister for Education, Employment and Workplace Relations, fulfilling all of her political aspirations.

The Rudd government was initially an exceptionally popular one. Then it wasn't. Polling in late 2009 and early

2010 indicated that both the federal government and Rudd personally were haemorrhaging approval due to some big policy swings that either resulted in legislation that was not passed or serious pushback from powerful bodies such as mining companies and media organisations. An election loomed later in 2010, and some in Labor believed that if Rudd remained leader, the new opposition leader Tony Abbott would become prime minister. Many were concerned about Rudd's leadership style and the fact he did not seem able to deal with the government's mounting political problems. Inevitably, there were whispers about whether a change of leader would improve things, and that meant pitting Julia Gillard, an unmarried former trade union lawyer, against Tony Abbott, a conservative Catholic.

On 24 June 2010, a leadership spill installed Julia Gillard as the leader of the Labor Party. Later that day, she was sworn in as Australia's first female prime minister. Less than two months later, the federal election resulted in political gridlock.

Julia Gillard's Labor government had won seventy-two seats in the House of Representatives, as had Tony Abbott's Coalition opposition. Six seats were won by crossbenchers, two of whom supported Labor and two supported the Coalition, which meant that two independents – Rob Oakeshott and Tony Windsor – were left as kingmakers, or perhaps queenmakers.

*

'I'm sure doctors can't stand watching medical shows,' Julia told me, 'and I'm not very good watching political shows, because if you were truly trying to film a day in the life of a prime minster it would very likely end up being ... Here she is sitting at her desk. Here she is, twelve hours later, she's still sitting at her desk. What's she done? She's had a dozen meetings and has shifted a stack of papers that you couldn't move in one go from one side of the desk to the other, but every one of those briefings represents a major decision, but it's not really exciting TV. That's actually the job, then ... There's the part of the job that people most see, and that's giving the speeches, going into the community, engaging with media, going to parliamentary events, which are about uplifting those decisions into the nation's laws or uplifting those decisions into Australia's hearts and minds or a combination of both.'

Some leaders are energised by the public side of their work and some are depleted by the paperwork, the grunt work, but I don't think that's true of Julia. She may also be energised by public appearances, but I think she's more engaged and enriched by the policy-making. Throughout her political career, she may have kept her policy work in her back pocket in the way I always have my bowling – where I feel I have proved myself time and again – to concentrate on when the captaincy is getting rough.

*

In a famous nod to the scrutiny and pressure unique to the captaincy of the Australian Test team, John Howard once quipped he had the second-most important job in Australia. It is definitely a job that tests you. The level of scrutiny can become draining and, for periods of the year, there is no respite. It is all-encompassing. When you are on the field, your mind is on the game. When you are off the field, the last (and next) games are all anyone wants to talk about. It requires a huge mental capacity and focus to remain creative and positive ... and this on top of the usual physical exhaustion of a normal Test series. As captain, you have to ensure you are always fresh, always making good decisions, and always there for your players. It also never stops.

I was young in my first series as Test captain, learning how to be a new captain and a new father – balancing life-changing moments with a once-in-a lifetime opportunity, and not wanting to fail at either of them.

Then in 2023, the challenge of being the new, unproven captain was gone but that was a series with a new level of scrutiny and its fair share of controversy. England had reinvented themselves and were doing really well, and Australia was the best team in the world. It was a moment everyone had been waiting for for years, and there was a lot of media attention. Every match was 50:50 and then there was that run-out in the second Test. Everything came under the microscope – tactics, morals, just everything.

The series was more condensed than usual – five games in just six weeks. Twenty-five days of cricket in forty days.

With the travel, physical workload as well as attention, it was exhausting in a way I've never known before.

So, I was fascinated to ask Julia about her time in the 'second-most important job in Australia' (not that I believe that) and the challenges of such a high-profile role in the face of intense media scrutiny, especially when she had to forge a very different coalition to form government in the midst of controversy.

Before they declared their preferences between a Gillard- or Abbott-run government, the independents Tony Windsor and Rob Oakeshott wanted to be briefed by senior public servants, to assess the key policies of both parties, and to make decisions informed by what they believed the outcome would be if either party came to power. In 2010, after the indecisive election and before the independents declared, I think Julia took solace in the confidence she had in her homework. She told me, 'There wasn't a moment [after the election] when you weren't aware of the burden of what was happening, and that was always with you, but the pace of the discussion was not frenzied. I deliberately let it not become frenzied, and as a result they took a long time. But I thought if people felt pushed into corners and required to decide really quickly, it would get too stressful for everyone, and they wouldn't be able to deal with and think things through, so we gave people space and consequently we had some space ourselves.'

Julia stayed in Canberra, making herself and her team available to speak to the independents about policy. She said she was 'always there' for Oakeshott and Windsor but wasn't 'calling them at midnight'. Mostly she made her chief policy adviser, Ian Davidoff, available to both men at all times, giving them the policy material they needed to make their decisions. Her opponent chose to go back to Sydney. She said, 'I thought one of the errors Tony Abbott made in that period was that we [Labor leadership] all stayed in Canberra for seventeen days and he went home to Sydney for the weekend, and I think that was … I don't think it changed the outcome, but it was an unusual thing to do. You needed to be there.'

The outcome was, of course, that Oakeshott and Windsor backed a Labor government with Julia Gillard at its head.

*

Perception can be everything in politics. Politicians may be doing an excellent job, but if there's a public perception that they aren't, they're going to be in trouble. That's where the symbolic role of a leader comes in – shoring up support in the public eye to smooth the way for the work you'd like to get done.

In cricket, there's a scoreboard that says who played well and who didn't, who won and who lost. In politics, there are crude statistics that politicians can point to – like job numbers, inflation and defence spending – but for the most part the public understands successes and failures through intermediaries, mostly the media. And a decline in the public's trust in media and other intermediaries has led to a decline in trust in politics as well.

When a batter smashes you around the park for a double hundred, you have to go over, shake their hand and tell them your efforts weren't as good as theirs today, but you'll see them again tomorrow. In politics, things are different. In politics, there is a danger of denying reality and claiming failure as success.

Adversarial politics only works when undertaken on a stable foundation of fact, but in the media environment we're in now, anything can just be asserted as fact and then everyone moves on before those facts have been verified and discrepancies investigated. This means that adversarial politics can become unpalatable, with the public often unsure what to think.

At both a state and federal level, one of the most overtly adversarial parts of Australian politics is Question Time. It's also a model that Julia said 'has increasingly run out of road'. 'There's been a change in the trust equation, and I think we do have to find more ways of interacting with the public, and some of those old models are inappropriate because people just don't want to see people acting like that.' She added that the 'trust equation' was changing when she was in politics, and that in the time since she left there has been a rising 'lack of trust in democracy and … in institutions'.

Polling and other research consistently indicate that this is the case in Australia and across most of the democratic world. In November and December 2023, Ipsos conducted a poll looking at populism and anti-elitist nativism, and it found that half of Australians believe 'our society is broken' and that more than two-thirds believe 'Australia needs a strong leader to take the country back from the rich and powerful'. Half of those surveyed also said they think the nation needs a 'strong leader willing to break the rules'. Most concerning for the political class is that 57 per cent of respondents agreed that 'traditional parties and politicians don't care about people like me'.

Julia said that Canberra should consider reforms to address this slide of legitimacy. 'I wouldn't be surprised if, in the next ten or fifteen years, there are some significant transitions around not only our parliament but other parliaments around the world.'

Notably, there is more and more use being made in the United Kingdom and in local councils in Australia of citizens' juries, which are groups of voters chosen randomly, as trial juries are. These juries are tasked with coming together to learn about and discuss particular issues. Afterwards they each reach conclusions about what they think should happen and file reports to government or Parliament that may become policy or law. Julia advocated for such an approach in the climate change area in 2010 and thinks this approach and other potential innovations in democratic processes are worthy of consideration now.

There may come a day in which politicians will be judged by their ability to assemble a citizens' jury and translate their understanding of an issue into policy for the betterment of the country. But we're not at that place yet, and we certainly weren't in that place twenty years ago. Back then – and still today – if a representative wanted to thrive in Australian politics, they needed to have sharp elbows, a sharp tongue and the ability to go on the offensive in Parliament when needed. That was the game that Julia entered and one that she particularly wanted to master – and not only for herself. 'I wanted to show, in my political career, that women could thrive and come to dominate that adversarial environment. It's a proposition that was doubted then: whether women could hack it as hard as things get in Question Time. One of the things I showed was that I could hack it.'

One of the ways that leaders – especially young leaders like me – can fail is by getting hung up on one role of leadership to the exclusion of the others. In my experience, this can happen when someone gets in your ear about something you may have done wrong, or when the media questions an action you've taken, and you address it to the point of obsession, unbalancing your perspective.

As a leader, when there is valid criticism you have to accept it. And it's essential to try to see criticism for what it is: regardless of the criticism and any potentially required change to your behaviour or perspective, you have to see criticism in context and keep moving forward. You cannot be derailed by it.

Doubt is human instinct. It's in everyone's head all the time, but you can't completely ignore it, because often doubt is an invitation to change for the better. If you're a leader, you can't let doubt freeze you – you have to keep working, keep acting, keep executing until it's time to stop leading and step down.

In my first year as Test captain, I was new to the job and still finding my feet. Then, suddenly, a year was gone. I realised that I only had three to four years to do everything I wanted to do, and if I spent much longer warming to the role, half my time would be gone before I could even get there. A part of me is still going 'I don't know how to do this role', but I've learned in that time to have the confidence to believe people picked me as a captain for a reason, and so I have to make my decisions and trust they made the right choice.

Julia was pushed into that corner from day one, by having to win over the support of the independents, and I asked her if it was like they were holding a gun to her head. She said it was important to her to stay true to her beliefs and not to pander to whatever the independents wanted.

*

As Australia's first female prime minister, Julia Gillard was often treated differently to her male predecessors. A deference had been afforded previous prime ministers that sometimes wasn't given to her. She told me there was a 'ridiculous degree of reporting about what I was wearing' in the first few months of her government, and there were questions about her marital status. 'I thought it would be a frenzy for a while and it would wear itself out, and it would go to politics as normal.' But it never really did. She was even questioned at a Perth radio station about whether her then partner, Tim, was gay.

In March 2011, three thousand protesters gathered on the lawn in front of Parliament. They were vehemently against a recently announced price on carbon. Many of those assembled were directing their ire against the prime minister and calling for her resignation. In front of signs that said 'Ditch the Witch' and 'Ju-LIAR Bob Brown's BITCH', the opposition leader Tony Abbott addressed the crowd in solidarity. In a documentary released in 2015, Julia said she'd been shocked by the incident, saying: 'I really don't know why this wasn't a career-ending moment for Tony Abbott – sexism is no better than racism.' She spoke little about it at the time, however, as according to her she hadn't wanted to highlight that moment, not wanting her government to be defined by her gender.

Another infamous incident occurred in 2012. After remarking twice that Julia should be put in a chaff bag and 'thrown out to sea', the radio broadcaster Alan Jones got on stage at a fundraising event and said that her recently deceased father had 'died a few weeks ago of shame'. Julia told me, 'I was angry at a time when we as a family needed to be in our own zone, grieving in our way. I knew it would be a big, big thing, so I needed to contact my sister so she could tell our mother before all of this rained down from the media. I didn't know if the media would seek her out for comment, because they knew where she lived.'

'Alan Jones would not have wanted to meet my mother in that period,' Julia told me. 'She was in her eighties, but he wouldn't have walked away, that's for sure.'

Julia said the gendered and personal attacks were not only attacks on her but also emblematic of how women can be attacked in ways men may not be. Many women in and beyond Parliament raised this with her and her team because they were concerned the next generation of women would be put off politics. 'With my team, this group started thinking about ways to put a spotlight on women and the impact of having a woman as PM.' In addition, she said, 'Because I hadn't done any of the calling-out earlier it became harder to do it. If I did it then the media response would be, "She didn't do it then, why's she doing it now? She's only doing it now for a political reason, not because she's genuinely concerned about it."'

Then, on one parliamentary day, an immediate and unplanned opportunity came to speak on the topic of misogyny. About that speech, Julia said, 'If I had agreed to give a speech in a month's time at the Press Club about sexism, it couldn't have been the speech I ended up giving. It was really the happenstance of the day and the opportunity it gave me.'

The 'misogyny speech' went viral and global. It is an iconic moment in our political history. But the happenstance and opportunity were, in fact, a moment of crisis for the Gillard government.

For four years, a Labor MP named Craig Thomson had been investigated by Fair Work Australia over allegations that he used his Health Services Union credit card for improper purposes. Thomson was suspended from the Labor Party, and in April 2012 he announced his intention to sit on the crossbench as an independent member of Parliament, putting Julia Gillard's minority government in jeopardy.

A few months later, another controversy threatened the strained calculus of the government. The Speaker of the House, Peter Slipper, was accused of sexual harassment and of misusing travel allowances. As the leader of the opposition, Tony Abbott used these allegations to attack the Gillard government, saying in Parliament that it was 'another day of shame for a government which should already have died of shame', echoing the comments made by Alan Jones. Julia told me, 'The events around Peter Slipper gave me an instant opportunity to give a speech on sexism and misogyny, and I hadn't expected to have the opportunity and I couldn't have created that opportunity.'

In response to a motion called for by Abbott for Slipper to be deposed as speaker, Julia Gillard began her famous speech with: 'I will not be lectured about sexism and misogyny by this man. I will not.' It was an eloquent speech full of fire, a strong tea brewed over months of gendered attacks.

\*

When I was just a few months into the role of captain, the contract for our coach, Justin Langer, was up for renewal. This process ended up being a drawn-out, public affair with everyone having an opinion. As captain, it wasn't my call whether his contract would be renewed or not, but my feedback was sought out by those decision makers. The feedback I gave was consistent: that we felt it was time for a change of direction.

When Justin's contract wasn't renewed, it put me right in the firing line. During the process I felt a real responsibility to be respectful of the process, and also to be open, transparent and honest, but always through the right avenues. I was never going to get caught up in the public firefight.

Like for Julia, a lot of the conversation was brought down to a low level – which had nothing to do with what was right or wrong for the team – and was distracted by ridiculous commentary and name-calling. Things snowballed in the media, but what I find funny is that when the big things in the media end up being either incorrect you become desensitised to the hyperbole. I got through it by remembering that my job is to look after Australian cricket, not the ex-players. I learned from this time that regardless of what decision you make, you're going to upset some people. So it's best to focus on the people it might affect and look at what's best as a whole. Once you have gathered as much relevant information as you can to make the most effective, informed decision, you have to make the decision that holds to your values and with consequences that you can live with.

*

In February 2012 the previously deposed prime minister Kevin Rudd resigned his position as foreign minister and challenged Julia's leadership in an attempted leadership spill. After being soundly beaten, Rudd went into the political wilderness. But the Gillard government was in trouble in the polls. Rudd started building renewed support within the Labor Party. After Julia announced an early election that increasingly looked as though it would be a landslide victory for an Abbott-led Coalition government, a further Labor leadership spill was called in March 2013.

Julia won that unopposed. Then, with polls worsening, a third Labor leadership spill was conducted in June. Prior to the vote, Julia said that whoever lost should retire from parliament at the next election. It went Rudd's way 57–45. Determined not to fall into gender stereotypes, Julia gave her final speech to the media without shedding a tear.

Julia Gillard had served as the Prime Minister of Australia for three years and three days.

She broke a significant gender barrier, and her government passed more legislation per year than any other federal government in Australian electoral history, despite being a minority government with a fractured party. Some of that legislation was high-profile – such as the Clean Energy Bill 2011, the Minerals Resource Rent Tax, the National Disability Insurance Scheme, and education and fiscal reforms – and some was not, but all of it changed the country.

Julia told me she's proud of what she did for gender equality in Australia, and proud of the achievements of her government, not only in the policies they passed but also in the manner in which they governed. She said hers was a government that was flexible without being reactive, one that wasn't defined by distractions such as personal attacks on her or even the fact that many people in the country did not see her as their preferred prime minister. 'You can't carry that with you. You're aware of all of those things. You're obviously aware of public sentiment as diagnosed by political polling or more generally. You move around the public yourself, people say things. You're able to get a sense of public sentiment and how the media's running, if they're pro or against [something], if [this is] one of its feeding frenzies or not, and you can see all that, but you have to keep it on the periphery of your vision or you wouldn't have enough at the centre to get the job done.'

I told Julia I was especially impressed by her ability to stay calm when there were personal attacks made against her, her then partner, her gender and even her deceased father. I was impressed by her ability to put all of that to one side, put her head down and just get to work. She said, 'I wasn't angry. In a sense I couldn't focus on anything else, I could do the things I needed to do.' When I asked her how she managed to stop anger from clouding her judgement, she said she'd developed this ability during her first years in the workplace, employed as a junior industrial relations lawyer at Slater and Gordon. It was one of the first Australian law firms to offer a free first consultation.

'You had people literally queued out the door, and you saw them on a half-hourly cycle. People would come in, tell you about something that had gone wrong for them fifteen years earlier, and they were clearly obsessed about it every day since. Mostly they were things that employment law wouldn't address, and even if they were things the law might address, you really did want to say to them, "You can keep obsessing about this every day to the day you die or ... you know those lever-arch folders full of stuff that you painstakingly collected? You can rip those up."

'Having the experience of being with others who'd gotten themselves down a vortex, I guess I had a learning experience about not doing that to myself.'

This is such good advice, applicable not just to any leader but to any person. Anyone obsessing about a slight or injustice – perceived or real – is choosing to be potentially right instead of potentially happy. If they are a leader and they make that choice, then they're probably also choosing not to be effective.

In our interview, Julia also shared advice about leadership from a British political strategist named Alan Milburn. He suggested to her that she should 'find the time to write down the purpose of the government that you're leading'. She did that, distilling into two pages what she wanted her government to achieve and also how she wanted it to act in the pursuit of those achievements. 'That [document] became the central steadying thing for me,' Julia said. 'If there was too much noise, too much static, I'd get that [document] out.'

I took two things from speaking with Julia. One, I don't want to go into politics. Two, I was impressed at how strong she was in keeping the right team around her and keeping them to those central values. In cricket we talk about 'owning our own space'. We have a team of individuals and I want to be conscious of their individual training needs, giving them the space to thrive in their own way. The onus is still on the individual, but we are still working together and towards the same goal.

Julia managed to be across everything and own the decisions of her team, but nine out of ten times, she said, she'd trust they were the experts and go with their recommendation.

Too often leaders want to win, which is a very fine instinct. They can't *only* want to win, however. The manner in which someone wins is often as important as the outcome itself, in part because one day you won't be a leader anymore, but you will forever be left with the choices you made to get ahead.

\*

Julia Gillard retired from politics at fifty-two. Within months she went from running the country to being at home with not much on the calendar. There isn't a direct analogy between ending an international cricket career and ending a career in federal politics, but there are some similarities. Selfishly, one of the reasons I wanted to speak to Julia was to learn about her transition out of a high-profile career.

I asked her what the first day is like, waking up away from the thing you've dedicated much of your life to. Julia's advice to me was to take some time for myself; she said that if I was anything like her, I'd be flat on my back for a while. 'When you stop, your body gets you back for all the long hours, hard work and stress. [It was like when] you finally go on your Christmas holidays, and two days in you wake up with a sore throat, when you pushed it too hard at the end of the year. Really, across my political career, I pushed it too hard for fifteen years – when I stopped, every little niggle I was ignoring came back ferociously. I was weak as a kitten for weeks. I was like, "It's 8.30 [pm], I guess I might go to bed." It was like that for a few weeks.'

Immediately after leaving politics, Julia sat down to write her memoir, *My Story*. That helped with 'the discipline of thinking about what you're going to leave in the past and what you're going to take with you'. I reckon she's on to something there.

Julia said that after leaving politics she had to transition back to being able to represent herself only, not herself and her party. She added that she and all senior politicians have constraints on them that mean they can't speak freely in public when in office, and so they often end up speaking in a repetitive and well-drilled manner, sounding almost inhuman. 'They don't act like that because they're crazy, they do it because words matter. An incautious statement can cause economic chaos or a diplomatic reaction. And then there is the "gotcha" approach of media who will magnify tiny wording differences between you and a colleague or what you said today versus yesterday. If you miscalled that, you got smashed in the newspapers. It was so nitpicking that you ended up at a press conferences with the ability to speak with a part of your mind while another part was hearing you speak and calibrating any problems with what you're saying as you're saying it.' Julia told me that, after retiring, she slowly lost that second part. 'Steve Bracks used the example of "slowly taking off the armour", and that's a good expression,' she said. 'You don't take it off immediately, but you do slowly.'

Using her freer voice, Julia has hosted a successful female-focused podcast, *A Podcast of One's Own*, and written two more books: *Women and Leadership: Real Lives, Real Lessons*, co-authored by Ngozi Okonjo-Iweala, and *Not Now, Not Ever: Ten Years on from the Misogyny Speech*.

What Julia doesn't use her voice for is questioning the decisions of the current government. 'I made a firm vow to myself in 2013 that I wouldn't be in the day-to-day chatter, and I'm never in the day-to-day chatter.' Julia added that she's still involved in (and up to date with the latest research on) causes that she's passionate about, such as gender equality, women's leadership, education and mental health, but she rarely makes public comments about government policy. She'd rather let the next generation of leaders talk to that, and doesn't see it as helpful to Australia for her to comment. 'I still work hard, I still have a very full calendar. I don't have that adrenaline-thumping, walking-to-Question Time thing, the thump of your heartbeat in your ear – I don't have that anymore. I'm not the type of person who misses it either.'

At the top, you only have finite time to accomplish change before you have to step aside and let the next generation move the game along. And then, when you step away, as Julia said, it's important to truly step away. You can be a resource for the next lot of leaders, but you've had your go and you have to let them make the decisions.

I hope once my time is done, I will be able to take a step back and let the next generation take over just like Julia has.

# 4

## Sport is a place where we can all belong; Australia can be also

*A conversation with John Moriarty*

I BECAME A UNICEF AMBASSADOR IN 2022, AROUND the time Becky, gave birth to Albie. When Becky fell pregnant, we started thinking a lot about what would be needed for our child to succeed in life. Life can be a perilous journey for anyone, but it's hardest for those who are fighting from the moment they are born. I was born lucky – I was born to loving parents, and we lived in a home where protection, nutrition and education were guaranteed.

I knew my son would enjoy the same prenatal luck I'd had, but when Becky was pregnant I thought about all the kids born behind life's starting line. That was when I decided to become a volunteer for UNICEF, who have a mandate to 'advocate for the protection and promotion of the rights of children, to meet children's basic needs and to expand their opportunities to reach their full potential'.

Before I started working with UNICEF, I already had some understanding of the importance of early childhood programs. My mother was a passionate teacher who believed in the power of the levers of education. She explained to me that the older a student is, the larger the lever required to change outcomes. From experience and through education, Mum really believed in the unique opportunities and pitfalls that exist in the thousand days after conception, through to birth and on to the second birthday. When UNICEF gave me the opportunity to support an initiative that was highly attentive to the needs of kids in those first thousand days and beyond, I was excited.

The Indi Kindi program, delivered by Moriarty Foundation, supports early years development, education and health of Indigenous children from birth to five years in remote Northern Territory communities. After I helped fund the program for two years, I was invited to visit the program in the community of Borroloola, on the Gulf of Carpentaria. That visit gave me an opportunity not only to see the work being done by the educators of Indi Kindi, but also to learn about Moriarty Foundation's co-founder, John Moriarty, who first left the town more than eighty years earlier and has been living an incredibly inspiring life ever since.

After I returned to Sydney, I interviewed John at his place on the North Shore, sitting across from him and his wife and Foundation co-founder, Ros, with tea and cake on the table between us. As he spoke, I was consistently in awe of the fact that the Australia John grew up in and the Australia my son is growing up in are lands linked by just one lifetime.

\*

Located in the north-eastern part of the Northern Territory, abutting uninhabited islands that jut into the Gulf of Carpentaria, the town of Borroloola is remote. Or at least it seemed remote to me when I flew over more than a thousand kilometres of wide plains, brown rivers, and mountains of red and green to get there. Remoteness is a relative concept, however. I was born and bred in Sydney, but for the Indigenous mobs who have lived in this area for tens of thousands of years, Borroloola is the centre of their world. It's the place that has sculpted their culture, history, language and spirit.

In 1870, the Indigenous people around Borroloola had little interaction with Europeans until a cattle-herding track from Darwin to Queensland was established through the area. By 1885, the region had been seized by stockmen and their families, and Borroloola had been established as a rough-hewn frontier town. In the fifteen years after white settlers arrived, many of the local Indigenous people were killed.

In 1910, the state government created the office of Chief Protector of Aborigines, in part to try to stop the massacres of Indigenous peoples. Twenty years later, the chief protector filed a report saying that 710 Indigenous peoples were living in and around Borroloola, which was by then a town with a post office, a library, a general store and a popular pub owned by an Irish family, the O'Sheas. In 1937, the publican's cousin, a man named John Moriarty, joined them to work at the hotel. In the town he met a young Yanyuwa woman named Kathleen (Morr-my-bina), who gave birth to a baby boy in 1938.

On the birth registry, the boy took his father's name, even though it's unlikely John Moriarty Snr ever met his son. It was illegal for him to 'cohabit' with Kathleen. John Jnr had two other names, though: Kundereri, his Yanyuwa ceremonial name, and Jumbana, his bush name. The boy lived in his maternal grandparents' camp for the first four years of his life, speaking Yanyuwa and Marra and living a tribal life – until his mother was told that her son would have to go to a school run by white people.

In 1943, John Moriarty was sent to the Roper River Mission, a few hundred kilometres west. Then, in John's words, 'my mum came to pick me up, but I'd been taken away'. He had been taken from the mission to Alice Springs. From there he was placed on a train to Adelaide, and from Adelaide he was transported to Sydney and on to the town of Mulgoa, about sixty kilometres from the capital. John had become part of the Stolen Generations. In the government's estimation, he was a 'half-caste' – meaning a child born of one Indigenous parent and one white parent – and the law said he could be taken from his home forcibly so that he might be assimilated into 'white society'.

In Mulgoa he was placed in a parish home, under the care of house parents. John started at the town's school with other children who had been stolen, and he made friends with local boys. With them, John made spears and hunted in the creek behind the church. He told me that he didn't see his mother while in Mulgoa, but he once received a hand-crafted pandanus basket from her. This treasured item is now an exhibit in the National Museum of Australia in Canberra.

John lived in Mulgoa until he was eleven, when one day, he was told he was being moved again. 'I didn't want to go,' John told me. 'I had a nice bed and good meals. I was bawling my eyes out.' But after some of his schoolfriends travelled to Sydney to see him off, he once again disappeared into the unknown.

After a long train journey through New South Wales, Victoria and South Australia, John arrived in Adelaide, where he was taken to St Francis House on the coast near Port Adelaide. This was an Anglican home where Indigenous boys who had been stolen by the government lived with Indigenous boys whose parents had asked the church to board them there.

There were worse and far worse places to end up in after being stolen from your mother and culture, and John told me that St Francis was not one of the far worse destinations. History seems to agree, because many extraordinary men came from that home. Excellence often emerges in clusters of exceptional people as they push each other further than they may have been able to go alone. The boys at St Francis, it seems, pushed each other in sport and academics, and later in politics.

John's sport was soccer, with that calling found when he and some friends at St Francis were eating apricots near a pitch adjacent to the home. The South Australian junior soccer team was about to train there, and seeing the boys from St Francis, a coach came over to ask if they might like to play in a practice match.

Reports of the scores from that match vary from 8–0 to 12–0, but what's known is that the St Francis boys ran rings around the representative team. This isn't surprising considering that three of the best soccer players in the country would soon emerge from St Francis at the same time: Gordon Briscoe and Charlie Perkins – who also had white fathers and Aboriginal mothers, and who had been born in Alice Springs – and John Moriarty.

Watching the match between the St Francis boys and the state team was an official from the local side, the Adelaide Port Thistle Soccer Club. Afterwards the official approached John and asked him to join up. 'I told him, "No thank you, sir." He said, "If you play, I'll buy you a pair of boots," and I said, "Well in that case, thank you very much."'

During a Christmas break, John decided to try to find his mum. There was no official apparatus for Stolen Generation children to reconnect with their families then, but a friendly welfare officer helped plan a meeting between John and his mother in Alice Springs. They were to meet at the local telegraph station, known as The Bungalow, which was four kilometres north of the township and had been designated as an 'Aboriginal reserve'. This was the place where John's friends Gordon and Charlie had been born.

On Alice Spring's main street, the teenaged John noticed a woman staring at him. 'She walked straight across the road and came over to me, and she said, "Where are you from?" I said, "I'm from Borroloola." She said, "What's your name?" I said, "John Moriarty." She said, "I'm your mother." [My mum and I] just sat down, you know, in the gutter there and chatted.'

It had been more than a decade. There was a lot of love, but there were also questions to ask. John wanted to know why his mum hadn't come and found him. She explained that she couldn't, that the law hadn't allowed it. The law hadn't even allowed her to visit him in Sydney or Adelaide, as no Indigenous person could cross state lines without the express permission of the Chief Protector of Aborigines.

John's mum told her son that she was a 'ward of the state'. She pointed out that he was too.

Under the Constitution of Australia, drafted over a decade in the lead-up to Federation, two passages made Indigenous peoples legally distinct not only to white people but also to people of all other races. The first provided that 'in reckoning the numbers of people of the Commonwealth, or of a State or other part of the Commonwealth, Aboriginal natives shall not be counted', essentially stating that Indigenous peoples should not be considered citizens in the way any other people in Australia would be considered, and that they would not be catered for after census data was collected.

The other passage in the Constitution related to the states' rights, saying that the new federal government had the power to make laws that would be binding across the country with respect to all 'people of any race, other than the Aboriginal race in any state, for whom it was deemed necessary to make special laws'. This meant that state laws could supersede any federal law, but only when those laws related specifically to Indigenous peoples.

John told me that the conversation with his mum was a revelatory and important one. He was fifteen and hadn't really thought before about his relationship with the government, nor his legal status under the Constitution. Now he had to confront the reality that, in the eyes of the law and the Constitution, he was a second-class citizen.

John's mother wanted him to go with her from Alice Springs back to Borroloola to be with family. He told me he didn't want to do that. In the wet season, overlanding as they would be, there was no way of knowing how long it would take to get to Borroloola and then back to Adelaide, with the roads in and out at best untended dirt and at worst a boggy quagmire. John wanted to go back to the place where he told me he most felt a sense of citizenship: the soccer pitch.

Back in Adelaide, John was enticed to move from Adelaide Thistle to Adelaide Juventus, a team primarily made up of Italian players. He said that in the company of these Italians, and with opposition from clubs like Adelaide Croatia and Adelaide Budapest, he shared the kinship of the outsider. 'A lot of [the foreign-born players] were treated like Aboriginal people too: being called "immigrants", "wogs", "degos" and all this sort of stuff.'

At age fifteen, John was told he had to move on from St Francis. He decided he should have a trade, so he successfully applied for a fitting and turning apprenticeship at the local power station, where he tended to the site's boilers and turbines. He earned the standard apprentice's wage – three pounds, six shillings and ninepence – approximately a third of the average wage of the day.

He said that moment of being told to move on was a shock, and that he thought mostly of a life of security and safety. He was a footballing natural, but also a hard worker. It was a great combination. As a teenager he debuted in South Australia's first division, where he played against his friends Gordon Briscoe and Charlie Perkins. A healthy rivalry developed between Charlie, who was named South Australia's most valuable player in 1957, and John, who in 1959 was selected to be part of the national side, which was to be touring Hong Kong in 1960.

John was the first Indigenous man to be selected in the national side, but the honour of being the first Indigenous man to play in the national side would fall to Harry Williams ten years later. Before the 1960 tour, the Australian Soccer Football Association was deregistered by FIFA after the international body found that European players were competing in Australia without approval from clubs they had contracts with. The Australian national side was not allowed to compete internationally in 1960 and for three years afterwards.

John had about as exceptional a soccer career as an Australian could have in the fifties and early sixties. On the pitch, he was comfortable, confident and respected, but off the pitch he was rarely allowed to forget about the laws that applied only to him and his fellow Indigenous peoples.

John could excel on the pitch and be selected in state and national teams, but if he wanted to play interstate or internationally, he could only do so with a governmental dispensation. In many instances he could only go to the pub or a restaurant with his team-mates if he presented a 'white card', a qualification based on the South African 'honorary white' system affording non-whites the rights of whites if they promised to 'act like a white person'. John told me the limits he felt were not only legislated but also self-imposed, because he'd grown up without an inherent feeling of security.

One day, while John was in Perth playing for South Australia, he was approached by an English scout touring Australia. 'He said to me, "Arsenal, Tottenham and Everton would like you to go and play for them," and I said, "Oh, thank you. Thank you, sir, but I can't. I'm still doing my apprenticeship," and, well, I wanted to keep myself anchored with some security. And I thought I better finish my qualifications.' He also felt like he had to pay off a house that he'd bought. At that time only one Australian had ever played professional football in England, but John didn't feel like he could chase that dream. 'It felt that [going to England] might set me back a couple of years' worth of security and then that having that security is what I felt I needed.'

Gordon Briscoe and Charlie Perkins went over to England to try out for professional sides, and Charlie became the second Australian to play professionally in England. One of John's few regrets is that he didn't go to England and test himself against some of the best players in the world. He told me that, despite his sporting success, he felt an ever-present deficiency, a feeling of tenuousness that was lessened on the pitch but couldn't be completely erased.

In 1965, while John was playing a club game at Hindmarsh Oval, his football career abruptly ended. One moment he was setting himself up at the near post for an attempt at goal; the next he was writhing in agony on the ground after a collision with the keeper that left him with a dislocated kneecap and much of the cartilage torn. Afterwards he attempted corrective surgery, but knee surgery in the sixties was not what it is now. 'I played two more games, but it wasn't right. That was it. I was done.'

John was off the pitch permanently, which meant he was away from one of the only places where his humanity, worth and citizenship were fully recognised. Before his injury, he had put much of his time and effort towards playing football, and afterwards he had to find a new purpose.

At the time of John's injury, some Australians were challenging attitudes about Australia's treatment of Indigenous peoples. Many were questioning the racist language in the Constitution that was the foundation of racist laws. Some citizens, Indigenous and non-Indigenous, were calling for a change to the Constitution – but that could only come after a successful referendum. The 'yes' side needed a consensus, and for that they needed champions. They needed people who had lived the pain of the Stolen Generation's experience, and who could speak authentically and eloquently to black and white Australians about the experience.

This was a moment of opportunity for John. He had earned a home in football; he could have just stayed behind the scenes, continuing to put most of his energy into the sport he loved. I've seen that in retiring cricketers a hundred times over – they want to stay in the place where they feel comfortable, close to their former glories. I don't begrudge anyone who does that, and I think it's great whenever someone wants to give back to the game that has given them so much. I also very much respect people who charge into a second act after their sporting career, especially when that charge is into a passion that transcends sport.

*

During my interview with John in Sydney, three thoughts emerged in my mind. One was that the wound inflicted by white people on Indigenous peoples is still so fresh. For my generation, something like racism embedded into law and in the Constitution feels like a remnant of ancient history – but sitting with John, I had to think about the fact that a system of what amounts to apartheid was a reality in our country only a few decades ago.

Another thought I had was of how far we've come. Of course, there's still a long way to go, but at least our government isn't denying the agency and basic personhood of Indigenous peoples anymore.

My final thought was that the people who brought about that change are exceptional. In hindsight, it's easy to assume that we would have fought for changes that now seem obviously needed, but change is hard. Most change is resisted externally and also internally. Injustice is usually presented as normal and natural, and when we see injustice, we often also hear a voice inside telling us not to rock the boat. People who speak up for themselves and others are an exception, usually supported by other exceptional people, usually living in exceptional times. They are brave and they are essential.

\*

John Moriarty's knee injury happened in 1965, when Nina Simone's 'Mississippi Goddam' and Sam Cooke's 'A Change Is Gonna Come' could be heard on Australian radios; when Malcolm X and Martin Luther King Jnr had become household names; and when the US Civil Rights Movement had become the tip of a global spear of equality that was starting to shatter the white Australian perception that non-white people should be considered second-class citizens.

In 1962, legislation had passed giving all Indigenous peoples voting rights, something denied to many of them previously. In 1963, the Yolngu people of Arnhem Land had challenged – by way of the Yirrkala bark petitions – the proposal of a mining company to mine and, in the minds of Indigenous peoples, destroy their ancestral lands, which led to the first documentary recognition of Indigenous peoples' land ownership in Australian law. In 1964, the federal Labor Party, then in opposition, had announced it would support a referendum calling for a change in the racist language of the Constitution.

In 1965, Charlie Perkins, then a student at the University of Sydney, emulated the 1961 US Freedom Rides into the segregated US South by driving a busload of students into western New South Wales. The US Freedom Rides challenged states that refused to integrate bus services despite federal laws ordering them to do so; Charlie's ride challenged a ban by a Returned Services League club against Indigenous ex-servicemen attending the club, and local laws barring Indigenous children from public swimming pools. After the highly publicised ride, Charlie's name became synonymous in the eyes of the public with the growing Indigenous Rights Movement. John told me, 'Charlie was strongly involved … because he was a talker. We all accepted him as our leader in that way, you know.'

In 1964, John had co-founded the South Australian Aborigines Progressive Association with Malcolm Cooper, another St Francis boy and one who had been a champion Australian Rules footballer. That organisation later helped fund the Aboriginal Community Centre in South Australia, which was run by another former St Francis boy.

After John's injury, he grew far more heavily involved in the Indigenous Rights Movement, sometimes in the public eye and sometimes behind closed doors. He became the State Secretary of the Aborigines Progressive Association and later a member of the Federal Council for the Advancement of Aborigines and Torres Strait Islanders. The latter was the key body that petitioned state and federal governments to change laws that discriminated against Indigenous peoples while allowing their removal from their ancestral lands and the destruction of those lands.

In 1965, shortly after John's career-ending injury, members of this council were afforded a meeting with Prime Minister Harold Holt. This was integral to the government's decision to join the opposition in supporting a referendum on racist language in the Constitution. A bill was put to the House of Representatives to attempt to repeal section 127, regarding the counting of Indigenous peoples in Australia's citizenry, but not section 51, allowing the states to go beyond federal laws when making laws regarding Indigenous peoples. Without a change to this section, some Indigenous peoples could still have their rights limited due to the Constitution.

Activists filed a petition of more than a hundred thousand signatures calling for a change in both parts of the Constitution. John drove to Canberra to meet with the other members of the council and to join in their campaign for changes to section 51. The fight was a tough one because, as John told me, 'Not many people – black or white – were prepared to fight for Aborigines in those days.' He added that there was no shortage of instances in which white people told him that he and other Indigenous peoples should just be appreciative of what they were being offered. 'That's what kept me going because it was important that we get equality,' he said. '[And that Indigenous peoples had] opportunities that everyone else had in this country.'

In early 1967, Parliament established a referendum on sections 51 and 127 in the Constitution, and in May the following question was asked of the country: 'Do you approve the proposed law for the alteration of the Constitution entitled – "An Act to alter the Constitution so as to omit certain words relating to the People of the Aboriginal Race in any State and so that Aboriginals are to be counted in reckoning the Population"?'

In the lead-up to the referendum, John worked hard to achieve a 'yes'. He was involved in a massive media and public relations campaign that asked for the Australian public to do the right thing: to see Indigenous peoples like John Moriarty and his family as people like everybody else, and for the Australian Constitution to recognise that fact. On 27 May 1967, more than ninety per cent of voters indicated that they wanted the language in the Constitution changed.

'We fought long and hard for that, and it was great,' John told me. But he said that afterwards he understood just how much work there was still to do. That referendum victory was an important moment in Australia, but all it did at the time was remove racist language in the Constitution – it didn't immediately change any laws. For an activist like John, the experience was a bit like being selected in the Test team: significant and important, but only an invitation to do more work.

John said that the exhausting march towards the 1967 Referendum was the start of something, not the end, and that he had the stamina to keep going. 'Fighting for rights was in me, you see,' he said. 'It's still in me.'

This is another thing that struck me about John. He's experienced a lot – he's worked in sport, arts, trade and government – but his passion and purpose never really changed the whole time. Much like Julia Gillard, he is defined by something indescribable at his core, and it shapes everything he does. He knows what is right and wrong and he won't waver on that. Like John Bertrand and Julia Gillard, John Moriarty envisions a better future, and does what he can to usher it in a little sooner.

Like Julia, he's also all about action. Making a difference isn't necessarily all about advocacy or being symbolic all the time. John spends half his time now up in Borroloola, boots on the ground, trying to make a difference. He always has an eye on what he can do practically.

It's inspiring. In my work with Cricket for Climate, we've tried to replicate this attitude. We do some advocacy work, but we also want to make a difference through action – installing energy-efficient fridges or solar panels on the roofs of cricket clubs. One of the Indi Kindi programs also trains the teachers and provides a pathway for them to higher education through diplomas, creating an ecosystem that is self-sustaining.

\*

Back at the time of the 1967 referendum, John was either twenty-eight or twenty-nine years of age – a government official had given him the birthdate of April Fool's Day, but he told me that his actual birthdate might be 17 July. When we met, fifty-six years later, he was eighty-five, with an incredible life of accomplishment beyond his sporting achievements.

Before and after the referendum, John was studying a Bachelor of Fine Arts at Flinders University. He graduated in 1970, the first Indigenous person in South Australia to do so. Afterwards, at the request of the Whitlam Labor government, John moved to Canberra to take up a position at the newly created Department of Aboriginal Affairs.

Later John became the Director of the Office of Aboriginal Affairs for South Australia, and in that role he advanced significant land rights legislation as well as legislation relating to education, health and welfare in his state. Along the way he met a journalist, writer and rights campaigner named Ros Langham. They fell in love, married and had three children: Tim, James and Julia.

In 1983, Ros and John set up Balarinji Design and Strategy Studio, a trail-blazing business that promotes Indigenous design excellence. One of the studio's best-known projects is the Qantas-Balarinji Flying Art Series, six aircraft covered with Balarinji designs created by its studio and Indigenous artists.

The success of that business gave the Moriartys the opportunity to give back to the communities that John told me have fostered and nourished him. Moriarty Foundation was registered in 2011, and since then has developed two interrelated community-controlled initiatives under its umbrella of support.

One is John Moriarty Football, which uses football (soccer) to improve school engagement and promote resilience and physical health in children through in-school and after-school sessions, school holiday clinics, tournaments and scholarships. The second is Indi Kindi, which is run not only in Borroloola but also at nearby Robinson River, as well as in the Tennant Creek and Mungkarta communities in central Northern Territory. Indi Kindi's classrooms have no walls as it is taught outside on Country and blends a unique Aboriginal approach to pedagogy with the Australian Early Years Learning Framework. Driven by seventy staff members, the majority of them living in the community and Indigenous, the Foundation's programs benefit about two thousand Indigenous girls and boys a week.

In the structure of Moriarty Foundation's programs lies much of what, in an unstructured way, helped John Moriarty become the man he is. The programs use football as a centrepiece, with the sport giving the kids a place where they can exercise, feel self-worth and team-build, as well as encouraging them to go to school. The football training is fun, and the kids want to come along to both the school and beyond-school sessions. Before and afterwards, the kids can learn football skills, receive medical check-ups and treatment, and be fed nutritious meals. All sessions are run in a culturally cognisant way, meaning that the programs recognise that teaching kids in an Indigenous community is different to teaching them in another setting, with both unique complications and inimitable opportunities.

As we spoke about the Foundation, John's eyes lit up. I started to understand how he's kept the flame burning all these years – how he has not just survived but thrived. In his life, he has had to fight for rights that every person should have inherently. He was selected by our national soccer team to represent a country that refused to count him and many of his loved ones as people in a census, and denied them their right of movement and choice. He would have every right to be angry, yet there just isn't any anger in him. As I spoke with him, I was in awe of his sense of gratitude and grace.

John said he's seen people break under the weight of great iniquity, and that in those cases the break was not the fault of the carrier but the size of the load. Yet being right and being broken is scarcely better than just being broken. He told me that he decided to be sanguine and to forgive not only because he thinks that this is the most effective way to bring about change, but also as part of a survival mechanism. John added, 'Why should I allow myself to be destroyed by those sorts of attitudes? Why become negative? It'll spoil your life.'

John has been thrown so many things, but he doesn't hold any grudges. He just serenely puts one foot in front of the other, consistently striving to make the world a fairer place and ignoring the chatter of those who think his views are needlessly disruptive.

As I walked away from my time with John – a kind and happy man who has found purpose through service – I thought of the old saying: 'Before embarking on a journey of revenge, first dig two graves.' It occurred to me that John Moriarty's approach to life is the antithesis of that quote, and the embodiment of another old saying that 'compassion is a gift given twice'.

# 5

## Amateurs try; professionals prepare, adapt and execute

*A conversation with Dennis Lillee*

IF YOU'RE READING A BOOK THAT I'VE WRITTEN, THEN you probably don't need much of an introduction to DK Lillee.

Often described as one of the most complete bowlers of any era, Dennis Lillee was an integral part of multiple Australian cricket teams. He was a Wisden Cricketer of the Year and part of Australia's Test Team of the Century; he is a Member of the Order of the British Empire, a Member of the Order of Australia and one of the ten inaugural inductees to the Australian Cricket Hall of Fame. Dennis was a brilliant player and is a great coach, a fact I can attest to personally.

He's something else too: he's a total professional.

The Dennis I know is always prepared, always working, always thinking about possible eventualities. Before we sat down for this interview, he had taken notes of events, dates and facts that might be pertinent so we could have the best discussion possible. His professionalism is one of the reasons I wanted to include him in this book; a professionalism that is all the more impressive considering he came up in the game at a time when the words 'professional' didn't often precede 'cricketer'.

Growing up, my brothers and I would hear stories from our dad of Packer and Dennis and World Series Cricket. We'd watch old footage that occasionally came on of packed stadiums, the teams in their bright uniforms, and the crowds that sometimes rushed the field after a big win. Decades later and what comes through strongest is the buzz of excitement – the crowds look like they're absolutely loving it. As a kid, you always thought white ball cricket had always been, but I reckon that's the thing about innovation – it's so obvious once it's done, even if it's controversial at the time. The closest thing we've seen to this innovation is T20 cricket, and in my career a lot of people allude to the growth of T20 in the same light to what World Series Cricket was like back then.

Cricket is full of traditions – it's been around hundreds of years – and people are often very worried about change. That's the thing about change: if you don't make any change, you stay really stale. But there's also no guarantee that a change is going to work, and it's in that unknown where all the scepticism and push-back comes in.

I've heard lots of stories about how, in the late sixties and early seventies when Dennis started making representative teams, the culture around cricket was different to what it is now. Even at some of the highest levels of the game, it was fiercely competitive but not necessarily professional. On the pitch, the players did everything they could to win, but off the pitch, lives were lived. The players drank a lot, and some smoked, even during breaks of play. Training wasn't as rigorous as it is today, as players weren't full-time cricketers, and there weren't too many doing fitness and conditioning – not outside the season, anyway. Dennis was an exception.

'I was running laps and doing sprints and push-ups and sit-ups and all that,' he said. 'They thought I was mad. I wanted to get as fit as anything, but all the other blokes just wanted to sit around drinking piss.' Dennis noted that there's nothing wrong with doing so, adding that he loves a glass of wine or a beer as much as the next bloke, but he also said he'd been driven as a young man to see just how far he could take himself as a cricketer. He wanted to further his performance, body and game, and to that end he engaged a former teacher from his high school who was uniquely positioned to fill the role.

This teacher, Frank Pyke, had been a grade cricketer himself before working at Dennis's school, Belmont Senior High. After teaching there, Frank went to the United States, where he obtained a PhD in Exercise Physiology and Human Performance from Indiana University. He returned to Perth and became a professor at the newly opened Department of Physical Education and Recreation at the University of Western Australia.

Dennis said that Frank was an incredibly important figure in his life, and he feels exceptionally lucky that they found each other when they did. At that time, coming into the seventies, I reckon there were a lot of cricketers who would have liked to train the way Dennis did under Frank but few had the opportunity to do so. No club, state or national side put together strength and fitness training programs then, nor was there much by way of injury prevention and treatment.

Dennis told me that, even when players made the Australian Test side, the only support staff member that toured with them was a 'rubber', who 'wasn't a doctor or a physio or something' and 'wasn't that helpful'. 'He'd yank you around a bit until you'd say, "Fuck this." You'd have to get the phone book and find a physio, and off you go in a taxi at your own cost, pay for it and come back.'

Australian cricketers still have to make sacrifices to play at the highest level, but it's different to what guys like Dennis had to go through. It was expensive to be a first-class cricketer then. They had to pay for a lot of things like physio out of their own pockets, and most players had careers outside of cricket. Some workplaces were accommodating of the employees who wanted to play top-class cricket, but some weren't. 'If you wanted time off to play cricket, you had to get leave, and when you did that, the sarcasm came in,' said Dennis. 'It was hard. You had to put cricket above anything else, but you still had to do everything else.'

Dennis's drive never wavered, though. He'd loved the game ever since he and his grandfather started staying up late together to listen to live transmissions of Australian tours of England on a transistor radio, and he'd set his goals high.

In the seventies, Dennis was a teller at the Commonwealth Bank in Perth. He worked hard and did night courses in accountancy, hoping that he might have a career as a bank manager. He was at the bank when it was first announced that he'd been picked for an Australian side. His grandfather, a boxing coach whom Dennis credits with his mental and physical fitness, called to congratulate him. 'I went out from the tellers' box and got a relief guy to come in so I could talk to my grandfather at the accountants' desk. I was speaking for no longer than a minute when my boss went *whack* straight down on the telephone receiver. He said, "Get back to your box." I said, "You fucking do that again, mate, and you'll wear this," holding up the phone.' That wasn't the end of Dennis's career at the Commonwealth Bank, but he never got another good performance review afterwards.

*

Dennis joined the Australian Test side in 1971, playing in the last two Tests of a seven-Test Ashes series in Australia. He bowled decently in a series in which Australia failed to win a match. It was a few months later, when Australia toured England, that he became known as a fearsome bowler. Pace had never been an issue for Dennis, but in England he harnessed more of that speed and captured thirty-one Test wickets: a record then in an Ashes series.

Then Dennis started suffering injuries. In a series against Pakistan in Australia, and then on a tour of the West Indies, he began to feel immense pain when bowling. 'A lot of people thought I was staging it,' he said. 'I copped a bit of ribbing. Then they'd just tell you to stop bowling for a few days and try again. When it got worse they'd give you the horse needle, which was steroid injections, I guess.' He usually tried to play through the pain, but when he couldn't he went to the doctor. Eventually he was diagnosed with a stress fracture in his back. This was the first such diagnosis in cricket, and some believed it was the death-knell for the then twenty-four-year-old's career.

Dennis's career wasn't over, though, as he professionalised his rehabilitation the way he had his training. After spending time in plaster and in a corset to reset the bones in his back, he basically put his rehabilitation in the hands of Frank Pyke. He undertook a gruelling strength and fitness routine while also making changes to his bowling action to minimise the likelihood of further fractures.

Dennis did all the work required, paying for all his medical treatments himself, and returned for the 1974/75 Ashes series. Alongside Jeff Thomson, Dennis spearheaded the attack in a series that Australia won 4–1.

After clinching the series in Sydney, the players poured into the rooms for some beers. During those celebrations, Dennis said, a moment came that revealed a rift in the game between the players and those who controlled the game. 'The rooms were packed, and we didn't know who was who, but if they were in the room, we assumed that the captain or the manager had okayed it, so we assumed everyone was in the tent, you know? We were all on the squirt, and this bloke started asking me questions about stuff, like payment and stuff.'

In 1974, Dennis was – like every other player in the team – getting $200 a Test match as payment (equivalent to about $2200 now), without a contract, and the money only got paid if they played. These match fees were the only compensation paid to players in the national side.

In that Ashes series the players had watched the grounds fill with record crowds: ninety thousand spectators in Melbourne and fifty thousand in Sydney on multiple days. They knew the cash being generated by the games was significant. Yet the players were seeing almost none of it. Even if a player was picked for every Test, he would be earning less than the minimum wage from cricket.

The international players were also upset about how their cricket schedules were getting busier. Previously the Australian team had really only played England, with tours of places like the West Indies or India happening perhaps once or twice in a player's career. Now, with the advent of passenger jets, international tours were becoming more common. Every player wanted to represent Australia as often as they could, but they were finding it extremely hard to balance their professional, personal and cricketing lives.

There was an impasse and a fracture. The then Test captain, Ian Chappell, had been agitating on behalf of the players, trying to come to an agreement with the newly renamed Australian Cricket Board (now Cricket Australia) that would see the players have some say in the international schedule and some kind of remuneration review, but he was being fobbed off.

A lot of players believed the situation was untenable, but any gripes were only aired within team circles. Players rarely spoke to anyone about money and issues with the board, but Dennis did just that in the Sydney Cricket Ground rooms after winning the Ashes.

'Do you think you're underpaid?' the man asked.

Dennis replied that he thought he was.

'How much do you think you should be paid?' the man asked.

Dennis considered his investment in the game and the revenue he and the other high-profile players were bringing in, and then answered, '$30,000 a year.' (That's about $330,000 a year now.)

Unbeknown to Dennis, the man was a journalist.

Dennis had no idea he'd contributed to a story until two days later, when he was in Perth playing grade cricket. He saw a man in a suit watching on – which, Dennis told me, was an unusual occurrence. After taking a better look, Dennis said he faintly recognised the man: an Australian Cricket Board member who had recently toured with the Test team. Dennis knew that he lived in Melbourne. 'He sort of waved, and I waved back. I walked over and asked, "What are you doing?" He said, "I want to have a chat to you afterwards," and I said, "Okay. See you in the bar afterwards."'

This is how Dennis remembers the conversation at the bar:

'You're a long way from home,' he said to the board member.

'Dennis, I'm here as a friend.'

'That's nice. You here on holiday?'

'No … Dennis, you have to be careful about things like what you've said in the paper. You know things like that can end badly.'

Dennis told me that he should have asked whether he was being threatened, but he just said, 'I'll say what I like.'

'As a friend, I thought I'd warn you,' the man replied.

And that was it. The conversation was over. The issue was far from resolved, however.

*

The Australian players were not going to continue as they had before. Dennis said each player had his own issue, but for him a major grievance was that he wasn't being treated like the professional he was. He said the board considered the players to be interchangeable, not recognising just how hard cricketers like him had worked to be successful and, in turn, marketable. 'The fans came to see us play,' Dennis said. 'Not the board or the CEO or anything. That should mean something.'

Dennis discussed the issue with his manager, John Cornell, who also managed Paul Hogan and appeared on screen as Hogan's offsider 'Strop' in *The Paul Hogan Show*. The pair came up with what they saw as a modest proposal: they might play a one-off one-day match against the rest of the world, with the gate and TV revenue going to the players of both teams. The other Australian players were interested.

But before taking it to the Australian Cricket Board, Cornell, with his business partner Austin Robertson, took the idea to Kerry Packer, the formidable owner of Channel Nine, which aired *The Paul Hogan Show*.

If you don't know of Kerry Packer, there's no brief way to introduce him. He was an Australian business and media titan, as powerful as any person in the country and with a personality of hammered steel. He never suffered fools lightly, never left a dollar on the table and never rented things he thought he could own.

Packer had been watching cricket's television ratings go up and up, and he badly wanted the rights for Nine. He had previously approached the Australian Cricket Board with a $2.5 million offer but been told they had already promised rights to the ABC for three years for $207,000. When Cornell, Robertson and Dennis approached Packer, the mogul saw an opportunity.

Starting with Dennis, Packer started secretly signing cricketers for a breakaway competition set to begin in 1977. Nearly every high-profile player in the Australian Test side, as well as the biggest names from overseas (the English, West Indian and subcontinental players earned no more than their Australian counterparts), signed up; Dennis told me that he doesn't know of any player who refused. 'I couldn't hold down a full-time job and play cricket, so for me it was [about] security. I had only a few more years, and we needed some sort of security. I didn't have a job. I had to start my own businesses, and I wanted some security in my life.'

All up, fifty players were signed to what was to be called 'World Series Cricket'. Planning began for six Tests and six one-day matches between Australia and the Rest of the World, with all of them to be broadcast on Nine.

Then, in May 1977, as the Australian team prepared in England for the first Ashes Test, the story broke. The players who had signed a contract with Packer were nearly immediately banned from any cricket venues associated with the Australian Cricket Board or the International Cricket Conference (the international body governing the game, now called the International Cricket Council). For players like Dennis, there was a real prospect that the breakaway competition might die on the vine and preclude them from ever playing first-class cricket again.

Across the world, the media screamed about the cricket 'circus' decrying the 'Test pirates'. With establishment figures and Packer's media enemies steadfastly, loudly and ideologically against the idea of World Series Cricket, initially there wasn't a lot of public support for the players. 'They thought we were being selfish and chasing a dollar,' said Dennis. 'That was how people saw it.' He explained that this perception spread to players who were outside Packer's largesse, describing a moment after the story had broken when he bumped into the wicketkeeper of his club side in the supermarket; the man wouldn't even meet Dennis's eyes when the player approached him. 'That's how raw it got,' Dennis told me. 'It wasn't a good time, but we believed in what we were doing.'

As Dennis told me his story, I couldn't help but think how isolating this must have been for him. Dennis was used to being loved by the public, playing in front of big crowds and spending his time in teams. But the true price of playing for Australia hadn't been seen by the public. As the crowds, ticket sales and workload grew, so too did the trade-offs for the players, until it became unsustainable.

Dennis and many of the World Series players wanted to change their own circumstances, but they also wanted to protect the future of the sport. Cricket was becoming increasingly popular, competitive and lucrative. The cricket boards wanted players who were professional and hardworking, but also endlessly available, with no concern for what that might mean to the men. Dennis was worried that some of the best players might simply leave the game. 'We thought of the game and also players in the future, because it was going to benefit players like yourself in the future,' Dennis told me. 'It was going to be tough, but we knew we had to do it.' He also told me how he felt he had nothing to lose in going for it. He'd already lost his bank-teller job, income and security because of the time he'd devoted to cricket.

Packer recognised the importance of consulting with the players in a way Dennis said the Australian Cricket Board never did. The media titan would call him regularly about competition formats, rule changes and potential signings. Once, Dennis and Chappell said they thought Ashley Mallett should get a World Series contract, but Packer told the pair Mallett simply couldn't bowl. When the men couldn't agree,

Packer decided to put the pads on and let Mallett bowl at him. After the player took Packer's wicket, he was offered a contract.

Packer was hands-on in every aspect of the competition because he, like Dennis, was a professional. No stone was left unturned in launching World Series Cricket, no question unanswered, no dollar spared but no cent wasted either. Dennis told me about a time when a game was abandoned during a rain shower, and Packer personally berated the umpires because the match ball was left to be waterlogged. 'He was a hard man but a good man,' Dennis said. 'He was good to me, anyway, and good for cricket.'

In the lead-up to the first World Series games, none of the players contracted to Packer could use any official cricket ground. For Dennis that meant not only were the WACA and grade cricket grounds off limits, but schools and local ovals also. Dennis told me, 'We had to use bloody playgrounds and parks to practise.'

The first season of World Series Cricket was a flop. There were 'Supertests' involving a full-strength West Indian team and one-day matches in the 'International Cup', but all were played primarily on grounds designed for Australian Rules football or on temporary drop-in pitches. Sometimes the contests seemed ad hoc and the crowds were meagre.

After a ruling in the British High Court, the players from the breakaway group were allowed back into their first-class sides – but few returned, as their welcome was far from certain and some cricket associations were still steadfastly against the players Packer had signed. 'We were unwavering, though,' said Dennis. More importantly, Packer was unwavering also. 'He was the only bloke that could have made it work because he was so strong and wouldn't wilt under pressure, and he got some pressure. He had a strong bunch of guys with him that were never going to wilt. A lot of people owe Kerry Packer a debt. He was a great man.'

Before the next World Series season began, tempers ran even higher, especially in England. When the competition had launched, the International Cricket Conference had been in lockstep with the national bodies – including the Australian, English, West Indian, Pakistani and Indian boards – but now a fraying came into effect.

England stayed steadfast. The Marylebone Cricket Club (now the England and Wales Cricket Board) was financially stable and supported, with British press outlets uniformly saying that what the boorish Australian businessman was doing to '*our*' game simply wasn't cricket. But this wasn't the case for many other national bodies. The West Indians were fearful of a report that World Series Cricket might soon be played in the Caribbean, the Australian body saw further attrition into its ranks as Packer signed younger players, and to field competitive sides India and Pakistan had to include World Series players in their national sides. Quietly, many of the national bodies asked the ICC for a reconciliation – and I'm sure the ICC was hoping that the second season would be a flop and that Kerry Packer would just cut his losses and run.

That didn't happen. Before the start of that season, there was renewed interest in the competition. In rural centres, some of Packer's secondary players had participated in a 'Country Cup' to enthusiastic crowds, while one of the most famous advertisements in Australian sport rolled out across Channel Nine programming, using the famous jingle 'C'mon Aussie C'mon'.

It was on 28 November 1978 that Dennis realised the competition had succeeded and the game had been forever changed. As the breakaway Australian and West Indian teams prepared for cricket's first day/night game since a novelty game decades earlier, John Cornell appeared in the rooms, telling Dennis to come with him to the balcony. When Dennis looked down, he saw lines into the gate that were a kilometre long. 'We've won,' Cornell said at the time. 'And we had,' Dennis told me. Eventually Packer ordered that the gates be opened so the match might start on time – and as a reward to the fans who were supporting his competition. Australia won the match easily, with Dennis taking four wickets for thirteen runs.

Six months later, an agreement had been reached between Packer and the Australian Cricket Board. World Series Cricket was dead. For the board, they would get back control of the game; for Packer, Channel Nine would have exclusive rights to telecast games in Australia, as well as a ten-year contract to promote and market cricket through his new company, PBL Marketing.

And for the players? They weren't sure. When the deal was announced, the contracted Australian players were in the West Indies and not directly involved in negotiations.

They wanted to return to the fold but didn't want to return to the situation they'd been in before Packer's intervention. The breakaway Aussies started their own negotiations with the board, and slowly but surely they made their way back into the Australian side.

Initially Dennis and his fellow professional cricketers wanted to set up a players' association like the one that Australia's professional tennis players were part of, but the Australian Cricket Board said that players unionising was something they would never support. (The Australian Cricketers Association was eventually established in 1997.)

A professionalising of the game was underway, and the players' role in that process had been elevated. With Kerry Packer now promoting and televising cricket, far more money came into the game, with some of it going into the players' pockets. Cricketers across Australia and the world were able to quit their jobs and concentrate on the game, something that I believe revolutionised the way cricket is played.

You might think, from all the talk about remuneration and fair pay, that money was a core narrative in my chat with Dennis. But the funny thing is, it barely came up. What came through wasn't about money, it was about seeing a better way of doing things.

World Series Cricket was a good and necessary change, not only for the players but for the game too. It reset some of the traditions and conventions that had held the game back and allowed it to become the exciting, international, future-focused sport that it is now.

A lot of people view the emergence of T20 cricket now in the same way as World Series was viewed in Dennis's day. Night play, red or pink balls, bright uniforms. For some people this is too much change, for others they are necessary innovation. People still want boring batters in T20 cricket, even though it's a format where you really have to go for it. For them, it simply isn't cricket without them.

There's a middle ground there somewhere. You have to change or you will become stagnant, but you don't want to change so much that you become unrecognisable. The key is, as it was with John Bertrand's innovative approaches, to be open-minded.

This opinion is pretty commonly held in the cricketing world, but we do sometimes forget that it wasn't the consensus opinion during and even after the reconciliation. 'We were treated like lepers by all the establishment,' said Dennis. 'Not just cricket but [the] establishment generally, people on the street, for a couple of years. Every current player should bear a thought for Packer and the players who stuck their necks out and were originally banned from all cricket.'

Like John Moriarty, Dennis had a core sense of what was right and wrong, and he followed that path unwaveringly. Like John Bertrand, he was also willing to try something that hadn't been done before, and trust himself to do something different. He took his career into his own hands and he was a trailblazer on the field in the way he approached his own game and looked after his body, but also for his part in the development of World Series Cricket, which changed the sport for the better forever.

\*

I became a professional cricketer at the start of 2011, and that's a summer I'll never forget. One day I was finishing school and getting ready for uni, the next I was debuting in first-grade cricket, then debuting in the New South Wales side, then in Big Bash cricket. It all happened in a flash, and all before I could legally have a beer.

In May 2011 I celebrated my eighteenth birthday, and then I was looking forward to more cricket, hopefully for New South Wales. A month later I was shocked to hear that Cricket Australia were offering me a contract. In November 2011 I was in South Africa, getting my baggy green from Ricky Ponting after some good form in T20 and One Day games, and after Ryan Harris suffered an injury.

Getting that first Test cap was like being in a dream. I'd been a skinny grommet slashing around with my brothers in the backyard – and then, all of a sudden, I was playing for Australia in a Test match. My debut in Johannesburg was a dream also: I got six wickets in the second innings, scored the winning runs and was named Player of the Match.

Alongside that dream, however, was a thin vein of cold reality. As I bowled in the first innings, a pain developed in my foot. It got worse with each day's play and each spell of bowling. After the match I had a searing pain in my heel, but

I thought it was caused by bruising that would improve with ice and time. This wasn't the case. I was diagnosed with a rupture of the fat pad in my heel and also with a bone stress injury.

That was the beginning of a very tough period in which I took one step forward and two steps back for years. After being sidelined for the entire 2011/12 home summer, I managed to return to cricket – for Australia's under-nineteens side – in April 2012. I then played for Australia in the T20 World Cup and for the Sydney Sixers in the T20 Champions League. Before I could get back in the Test side, however, I broke down again. I had some scans to try to locate the cause of the pain I was experiencing in my back; they revealed I had stress fractures. I'd be out of cricket for at least the Australian summer.

It was a time of immense frustration. I knew I could play against the best players around, and I desperately wanted to keep testing my skills against theirs, but every time I got a few games together or a good run of training, some injury or diagnosis dragged me back to square one.

Advice came thick and fast. In 2012, I started to try to remodel my bowling action. Some coaches had suggested that this might limit the likelihood of future injuries and get me back onto the pitch. I was often told to bowl through it, which I tried to do, but I did so with pain, unable to even bend over to tie my shoelaces.

I ended up not liking my cricket that much. I'm not a technician as a cricketer: I'm a competitor. I'd never been much of a nets bowler at the best of times, and the mundanity of bowling in the nets, not knowing when I was going to play again, was not my idea of fun. It was like I was learning to walk again from scratch. I did it, though, bowling and bowling and bowling, trying to find a new action that would work. But as I did that, it felt like I was just getting worse; like I was losing what I thought had made me a good bowler. I felt like I was losing the bounce and accuracy – and ten or so kilometres of pace – that were my strengths.

I became pretty dispirited. I was still young and had a lot of cricket ahead of me if I stayed available, but I wondered if I'd always struggle with injuries, spending my career doing the part of cricket that I don't enjoy that much – bowling in the nets and working in the weights room – without consistently enjoying the part of the game that I love: competition.

In any sport, the best ability is availability, and I wondered whether I'd ever show the consistency and availability required to be picked consistently for Australia. Then my manager, Neil Maxwell, made a suggestion to me. He said I should go to Perth and do some sessions with Dennis, who Maxxy said had helped Brett Lee immensely.

Since retiring from professional cricket, Dennis had become a legendary coach, mostly due to coaching that he'd done in India for an organisation called the MRF Pace Foundation. This foundation had been established in 1987 by Ravi Mammen, the managing director of a company called the Madras Rubber Factory and also a massive cricket fan. Mammen was a wealthy businessman who wanted to be a benefactor for Indian cricket, believing the best way he could do that was to develop fast bowlers for a national side that was usually weighted towards spin bowling. To that end he wanted Dennis's help. Dennis became the director of the MRF Pace Foundation, drumming into the Indian players a dedication to fitness, core strength and diet, as well as tactics and bowling fundamentals.

Multiple generations of great fast bowlers went through the MRF Pace Foundation, and not only Indian players. Brett Lee's time with Dennis was at the foundation, and Glenn McGrath spent time training there also. By the time I started working with Dennis, he'd only just retired as the Foundation's director, having been replaced by McGrath. Dennis taught me a hell of a lot that was accessible and most importantly enduring, and I give him a lot of credit for the durability I've ended up having in my career.

In 2012, Dennis took me all the way back to the basics. We looked at the dynamics of my bowling, studying my run-up and then my approach, my action, my landing and follow-through. Dennis didn't want to be radical and tear the book up and start again. I already had an action and a successful one, Dennis could tell that, so he just wanted to see what changes could be applied. We tinkered and investigated whether there was any extraneous movement and, if so, where it started. Could it be eradicated or counterbalanced? Where was energy gathered and expended? How could I reduce some of the twisting, while still holding on to my strengths?

I guess this approach wasn't a million miles from the other coaching I was getting, but I enjoyed it more and took more from it because it felt like Dennis wasn't the only coach involved in the process. He didn't take a cookie-cutter approach to bowling either – working from the base of a safe action and expanding from there. Instead, he wanted to work from my strengths as a bowler and harness those, while finding some efficiencies. One of the base principles of his coaching ethos is that the player has to be their own coach, and that idea really resonated with me. Dennis taught me a lot, and the thing that he stressed while working with me and the thing I remember most vividly is that you have to be able to take advice from coaches like him and make it your own.

Some people respond differently to different coaches and players, and that's part of the direction to training I wanted to take the team - respecting their needs as individuals instead of taking a cookie-cutter approach. As a bowler, I can have high-level conversations with some of the batters, but maybe that's going to be better - or better received - coming from a coach who has been a batter for twenty years. Although this is not an admirable quality, I know I'm cynical of advice on technique from non-bowlers unless I think they know what they're talking about.

I've had great coaches who never played the game at the top levels, and I've seen great former players who weren't much chop as coaches, but there's nothing quite like a great player who is now a great coach. I reckon Dennis is one of those because he vividly remembers what it was like being a player but knows that he's not going to be out there on the pitch anymore.

A great coach doesn't rant and rave; they instil in their players a sense of personal responsibility. The cricketers have to play the game, to fight for their successes and accept their failures, and no coach – or administrator, commentator or fan, for that matter – can do that for them. You can get all the advice in the world from trusted professionals, and a lot of that advice cancels each other out, so in the end it is about the individual to trust themselves and steer their own path. I took a lot from Dennis, and he helped me really get my career going, but one of the most important things I took away was his idea of what it means to be a player who takes responsibility.

My bowling did change when I was working with Dennis, and mercifully I haven't continued to suffer the chain of injuries that I did when my career started, but my perspective changed too. People like Dennis Lillee are in a continuum of the continued improvement of the game, improvements that I have benefited from. I hope to be part of that continuum, and I hope one day I'll be able to help some other young cricketers when they're preparing to be out in the middle.

\*

Cricket kept moving after Kerry Packer's intervention, expanding, modernising and changing. In the eighties and nineties, more countries reached the top level of the game.

One-day cricket became more popular, then T20 cricket. Cable and satellite television fed that popularity. This all meant more interest, more travel and more money. The way the game was governed needed to change, along with how the players were paid and represented.

In the mid-nineties, another disparity between pay and revenue emerged. It wasn't as bad as the one that existed in 1974, but cricketers' pay rises were in no way commensurate with the revenue that was coming into the game. This meant most players had to try to keep up full-time jobs outside cricket, often using annual leave entitlements from these other jobs in order to play or tour. Support for injured players was limited, job security – as cricketers and in their other careers – wasn't there, nor was there any assistance for past players or female cricketers.

It's estimated that in the late nineties, Australian player payments represented about nine per cent of all revenue generated by their games, with many of the state players not even being paid to play in games that were televised and made money at the gate. This disparity would have been addressed well before the nineties if professional cricketers had been allowed to bargain collectively, but this had been strictly forbidden by the Australian Cricket Board when the players came back into the fold after the deal between Packer and the Board in 1978.

In September 1997, every first-class cricketer signed up to have the Australian Cricketers Association work on their behalf to bargain for salaries and benefits. Furthermore, the Association created a charter saying they would act for players in employment disputes and administer an account for the payment of retirement or transitional benefits.

The first proposal for improved player conditions put forward by the Association was rejected outright, and a stalemate between the parties followed. Eventually, after a lot of heated meetings, the players landed a deal that they could only have negotiated as a group. Two major breakthroughs were achieved: one was that all male state players would now have guaranteed contracts, and the other was that the players would share a percentage of Australian cricket's revenue. More players would now be able to concentrate on the game, and furthermore, the top players would be partners in the growth of the game. As the game grew and as revenue increased, players would benefit financially; if somehow the game contracted and revenue decreased, they would feel it in the hip pocket. There have been changes in the pay structure since, too, including the much-needed inclusion of the professional women players.

This revenue-sharing model persists and is part of my current contract with Cricket Australia. The percentage is nowhere near what the American NBA and NFL players' associations have negotiated – both are at about fifty per cent – but I think the agreement we have is fair and equitable. It also generally puts the sport in a good position as it leaves ample money for administration, development and grassroots cricket, but also incentivises everyone to continue to grow the game together.

It's true that there is more money in the game than was imagined when the first revenue-sharing agreement was signed, thanks in no small part to India's economic rise and the success of the IPL. However, I don't think that is an argument against revenue sharing. For the game to thrive, you have to respect those playing at the top levels, both men and women, and recognise that they are essential to the sport's ongoing success. We are very lucky to have almost 300 professional male and female cricketers in Australia now. As a result, we have strong domestic competitions, Big Bash Leagues (women's and men's) that fans flock to, as well as the international summer of cricket. This all bodes well for fans of cricket in Australia, and provides us a great chance at sustained success on the global stage.

Dennis told me that he 'didn't play harder when [he] was being paid, nor play less hard when [he] wasn't'. That's true of me and almost all top players. A competitor competes, regardless of incentives.

My key takeaway from talking with Dennis was how he took control of his career, and left no stone unturned in his quest for greatness. Dennis really was a trail-blazer in how a fast bowler needs to train and condition their body to get the best out of themselves. He wouldn't settle for how things were already done and do the ordinary. He was happy to go about it in his own way to set himself up to be extraordinary. He had a healthy balance of respect for the experts and coaches in his corner, but enough confidence in his own judgement to filter through that advice and make use of that which suited him.

Another takeaway for me was how Dennis and the other World Series players professionalised the sport. Part of being a professional is being paid equitably, but another part is to be a custodian for future generations, and to ensure that we leave the game in a better place when we end our careers.

Dennis saw that the system was inequitable, and he fought for what he believed was fair – not just for himself but for those who would come after him. I think the players, the game and the fans are now all much better off for it.

We current players owe so much to the generation that came before us, and it's important that we continue to improve the sport for those in the future. Change can be uncomfortable, sometimes even scary. But just as we can hardly believe what cricket looked like before Dennis, maybe one day future generations will look back on cricket today and feel the same.

# 6

## Sometimes there is little difference between giving and taking

*A conversation with Shaun Christie-David*

COLOMBO SOCIAL SITS ON ENMORE ROAD, A BUZZY, hip street in Sydney's inner west. Across from the restaurant is a popular music venue, where Oasis and the Rolling Stones have played, and either side of Colombo Social are places where you can get a cocktail, an ice cream, some cheap dumplings or a fine-dining main. Colombo Social sits happily among it all. The restaurant is welcoming but also upscale. Music, mostly hip-hop, thrums along underneath a hubbub of conversation. The place has a great Australian and Sri Lankan vibe in the fit-out, the art on the walls and the aroma coming from the kitchen.

Its owner, Shaun Christie-David, is a modern Australian bloke: tall and broad, with a shaved head, a beard and an ever-present smile. He looks like a Sri Lankan James Harden. When he hosted me, he was welcoming and funny, and he made sure my wineglass always had something in it. On the surface, he looks like a successful restaurateur, living the hospitality dream. And he is that, but he's also a social entrepreneur. That's basically the same as being a regular entrepreneur, except that the last line of his balance sheet doesn't have a dollar sign. Shaun's businesses have to make money, but they don't exist to make money. The stated purpose of his businesses is the creation of social capital: feeding those who can't feed themselves, giving jobs to people who can't find other work, and instilling a sense of pride in people who have done it tough.

So far, Shaun's businesses have donated more than half a million meals in Australia and across the world. He employs close to 200 staff who would otherwise have had to rely on government benefits and charity themselves. There are also intangible benefits on that bottom line, such as the feeling of being part of a community. These are the benefits enjoyed by (among many others) Ukrainian refugees who have fled the war, Sri Lankan political refugees in Australia on bridging visas, and minors in youth detention who now have a career pathway when they're released. These benefits are also enjoyed by people sleeping rough in inner-city Sydney, who know that there's a crew nearby making them a meal that won't just bring sustenance but also pleasure. Those benefits exist as far afield as Afghanistan, Sri Lanka and Ukraine.

There have also been intangible benefits to one finance bro – shaved head, big beard, bigger smile – who was on a path that would have been comfortable and financially stable for a while, but was ultimately unsustainable. 'I thought I was going to have a fun, boozy life.' Shaun laughed. 'I never thought I'd end up running a charity.'

Shaun was born in Australia in 1986. One of his two older brothers was born in Sri Lanka, and the other was born in Saudi Arabia, where their dad, Clement, was working as a mechanical engineer for a US company. He and Shaun's mum, Shiranie, are Sri Lankan, his mum from Batticaloa on that country's east coast, his dad from Colombo, and they moved to Saudi Arabia in the seventies because of the economic opportunities the kingdom offered them. While they were there, a civil war erupted back home between ethnically Tamil militia groups and the Sri Lankan armed forces, which was overwhelmingly Sinhalese. Shaun's family are Tamil and they were persecuted when violence broke out.

This left Shaun's parents and brothers between a rock and a hard place. To go back to Sri Lanka would be to return to a war zone and an uncertain future, but to stay in Saudi Arabia would be to commit to an uncertain future as refugees, never gaining citizenship and being beholden to what, to them, were unusual and restrictive laws and customs. Shaun told me, 'Then my aunt was like, "I'm living in this place called Australia. It's amazing. You don't understand how great it is in this country. You don't understand the opportunities, you don't understand how well people treat you. You gotta get out here.'"

Eventually the family was sponsored to come to Sydney, where they settled in the suburb of Bankstown, in the city's south-west. A year after they arrived, Shaun was born.

Shaun said that when he was growing up, there were a few ways his and his brothers' lives in Sydney reached across to their parents' homeland. One was through family, of course, with a large cohort of aunties, uncles and cousins presenting for special occasions like Christmas. Another was through cricket, a game Shaun's dad had played as a boy. He encouraged his boys to play in junior club cricket and also in tournaments that he arranged, where Sri Lankan-Australian kids coming from both Tamil and Sinhalese backgrounds could play together. Shaun told me his older brothers were very good cricketers, but he was 'truly awful' – never knowing the score but always safe in the knowledge that it didn't matter much because his team would lose anyway.

Shaun is also tethered to Sri Lanka through food. His mother is an exceptional home cook, making curries and dhals from recipes passed down for generations. She has often been tasked with catering extended family gatherings that, Shaun said, have sometimes numbered in the triple digits.

Despite this, Shaun says he didn't really feel that Sri Lankan growing up. Currently there are about twenty thousand people of Sri Lankan heritage in New South Wales, but when the Christie-David family arrived in the eighties, there were very few. According to Shaun, in south-western Sydney there were a jumble of ethnicities, nationalities and cultures. One of those ethnicities was Tamil and one of those nationalities was Sri Lankan, but he said neither identity was particularly dominant for him. He told me there were times when he actively resisted his heritage. 'Mum used to make these amazing dhal sandwiches for me to take to school, and I just used to throw them in the bin. I just wanted Vegemite like the other kids. I mean, those dhal sandwiches are delicious. What was I thinking?'

Shaun can identify the exact moment when he knew he wanted to work in finance. About twenty years ago, he and his family went to Martin Place, the financial heart of Sydney's CBD, so his older brother could be interviewed for a job. For young Shaun, Martin Place was full of otherworldly characters. 'There were all these people wearing suits, walking with purpose,' he said. 'Everyone seemed so busy and important. I was like, *I really want to be busy and important.*'

Shaun 'studied his arse off' in primary school to get into a selective high school and, from there, studied his arse off in high school, then again at university as he completed his business and finance degree. Afterwards he was employed in finance in the CBD, first at the Royal Bank of Canada, then at Perpetual Limited, and finally at Macquarie Bank, where he worked at their Martin Place offices. 'It was a good career, and the money was what you'd expect,' said Shaun. Yet, he added, he never really settled into his suits.

He said part of his discomfort in finance was racial. In all of his finance roles, he told me, it was rare for him to work alongside anyone who wasn't white. He said his discomfort didn't necessarily come from overt racial discrimination – although he thinks he benefited from having an anglicised name – but there was a general disregard for racial sensitivity. This was highlighted in a moment when a client he'd only ever spoken to on the phone casually referred to American President Barack Obama with a racial slur.

Another aspect of discomfort was his socioeconomic background. 'There was this real badge of honour in finance about the private school you went to, you know, "North Shore this, we went to Knox, we went to Grammar." That kind of thing,' said Shaun, referencing the area where Sydney's established wealthy families primarily live, and two of Australia's oldest private schools. Shaun recalled a time at one of the banks when he was looking to hire someone, and his senior manager glanced over his shoulder at a resumé he was considering. His manager noticed the applicant had an Indian name and had gone to school in Campbelltown, in Sydney's west. 'She said, "Wrong side of the bridge, wrong last name,"' Shaun told me. 'She was saying that to *me*? It was very much like that. There were no brown people on the whole floor.'

Shaun managed to keep working, though. The work was intellectually stimulating, and he was earning a large salary, with a yearly bonus and a near-limitless corporate card to boot. As a boy he'd wanted to be busy and important, and now he seemed to be. There were questions in the back of his mind, though. Was he important? Was this work important? To the people around him, it seemed important, and he was being paid as though what he did was important … but was it? And if it was, then who was it important to?

There was another snag about the work, too: most of the people he worked with seemed miserable. And the more senior they were, the bigger the bonus they earned, but the more miserable they seemed. 'These people weren't happy, and they weren't moving towards a place where they might be happy in the future,' said Shaun. 'But I was like, *Maybe I'll just play the game and eventually I'll have enough money to, you know, to fill the void. If I go out and get, like, smashed every weekend, and then get up and go and make heaps of money, then maybe that will just make everything better.*'

Shaun kept working and earning until a moment of crisis arrived. In 2009, hostilities between the Tamil militia groups and Sinhalese armed forces ceased, and a peace agreement was signed. Afterwards, Shaun's family were at last able to return home to Sri Lanka, taking their first ever holiday together and flying into Sri Lanka's economic capital, Colombo, where one of Shaun's uncles and his family lived. Shaun told me this uncle wanted to warmly welcome his nephews, all of whom were now working in financial services roles, and to do so he'd arranged for Shaun and his brothers to spend a day at a tailor's shop. They were impressed by the tailor's craftsmanship and the fabrics he was using – and they were blown away by the price. 'The suits were like sixty [Australian] bucks each. We were like, "Awesome. Let's get ten."'

Working for the tailor was a group of fifteen-year-old Tamil boys, who were running around the shop, getting material, making preparations and getting refreshments for the Australians. 'I was just waiting,' said Shaun, 'and things got uncomfortable. These guys were making small talk, like, "Oh, where from, sir?" And I was like, "*Sir?*" These kids, who could never in their life afford a sixty-dollar suit, and there was no difference between me and them. None.

I'm not special, I'm not super smart or anything, I was just lucky. The only difference between them and me was that my parents made a decision to move to Australia. I didn't do shit, and yet I'm the sir? I was like, *If I was born here, I'd be doing this, and someone else would be standing there being called sir.* I was standing like an arrogant fuck, getting these suits that would basically cost nothing [to me] but that these kids could never, ever afford, and … everything just came crashing down around me. I was like, *What am I doing here? What am I doing with my life?* It was the worst feeling in the world. I was never the same person again.'

\*

Shaun believes that moment in Colombo was an acute experience of survivor's guilt, something he thinks his parents had been battling throughout their time in Australia.

They worked hard when they came to Australia. His father's qualifications as a mechanical engineer were not recognised in Australia, so he worked as a mobile mechanic. Rain, hail or blistering shine, every day he was under other people's cars. Shaun's parents weren't poor, but by Australian standards they weren't in a place of economic advantage. Yet they were in a privileged position in comparison to many of their friends and family members who were still in Sri Lanka. They had far more money, opportunity and safety than most people in Sri Lanka, and certainly most Tamils during the war.

Shaun said he thinks his parents felt guilty about their relative luck, but that he didn't recognise that guilt because of how hard they had to work and their place in the Australian economic hierarchy. He added that only as an adult did he recognise the tension they must have felt between the forces of fortune and misfortune when being transplanted from a poor home country to a rich new country. They were always thinking about home and the people who were still there, often sending money back when they could – but they were also thinking about their future and how to plan for it. 'I think my parents were like, *What do we do with this incredible opportunity of being in Australia? What's the right thing to do?*'

One thing Shaun's parents knew they wanted was for their sons to have opportunities. His dad strongly felt that he wanted his boys to work indoors, in an office. He worked outside, as did his friends; he was exhausted at the end of the day and developed rough, calloused hands – he wanted his boys to work differently. Shaun's mum just wanted her boys to stay close to her and live good lives. 'My mum will always say, like, "I'm never gonna judge you for how much money you have." Never meant anything to her. She'd say, "All I want is for you to take me out for a coffee every now and again. And that you do something with your life that is meaningful."'

In Colombo, buying tailored suits, Shaun feared he wasn't doing something meaningful with his life. He went back to work after that trip, but the feeling that he had to change his life and do something different never went away – until he changed his life and did something different. 'It took me five or six years to figure it out,' he said.

Initially his pivot away from finance was in the directions of media and Indigenous health. He wanted to do something that had a social good, but he also wanted it to be fun and not preachy. He wanted to do something that was personal too; being an Australian, he wanted his work to benefit Indigenous Australians. So Shaun – alongside some partners, including Australian broadcaster Dr Norman Swan – worked for five years under a federal government grant to create the Aboriginal Health Television Network, which used Indigenous voices and Indigenous languages to promote health literacy. 'I resigned [from the bank] the day we got the funding,' said Shaun.

Shaun said the plan was always to hand the network over to Indigenous owner–operators. After a few years, he worked his way out of the job and once again had to figure out what to do. Eventually he figured out that he wanted to open a restaurant, with a vision emerging of a Sri Lankan place that was nothing like any that already existed in Australia. There were good Sri Lankan restaurants in outer-Sydney suburbs such as Toongabbie and Flemington, but they were basically emulations of restaurants in Sri Lanka. 'They'd have plastic chairs and Sri Lankan music, and good food but a bit daggy,' said Shaun.

He wanted to set up a venue like the restaurants he'd taken clients to when he had his corporate card; like the restaurants he went to on dates. He conceived of a place that would have a cocktail menu like an inner-city bar and a hip-hop soundtrack emulating the music he and his friends listened to growing up. There would be Sri Lankan flavours but with a modern, fusion twist, as the Australian restaurant Chin Chin had done for Thai food and Ms.G's for Vietnamese. A mostly modern twist, anyway – the curries wouldn't be modern: they'd be made from the recipes handed down to his grandmother and mum. 'Perfection is just perfection,' Shaun said. 'You don't need to fuck with it.'

The restaurant would be a paean to his mum, but also representative of who he was and the people he'd grown up alongside. 'It was always going to be a first-generation migrant venue. It was for me, but it was for all the people who walk in two worlds.' It was going to be fun, it was going to be cool, and – in the initial conception of the first restaurant – it was going to be staffed with asylum seekers. Shaun couldn't hire the boys at the tailor's shop in Colombo, but he could hire people who'd come to Australia as his parents had, fleeing violence or persecution and ready to start a new journey.

He costed the business, put together a business plan and took the idea to a hospitality loan expert at a major bank, who was a friend of a friend. 'She literally laughed in my face,' said Shaun.

Shaun had no hospitality experience, and in the conception of his restaurant, few people working for him would either. The loan officer didn't believe he'd hit his earning targets and that 'he'd be lucky to get half of it'. She wasn't the only one, either. No one would back a business that Shaun was firmly convinced would work.

He told me, 'I've never cried in front of my parents before, but one day I started bawling. I had done so much work and was so convinced it would work.' His dad asked him to explain the business to him, and afterwards he offered to empty his superannuation account so he could become Shaun's financial backer. Colombo Social opened in November 2019 and became exactly what Shaun had conceived of, from the asylum-seeker staff, to the music and cocktails, to the Sri Lankan–inspired fit-out, to the fusion food and curries that had been perfected after his mum taught the chefs how to prepare them.

The opening ended up being more successful than anyone could have dreamed. There was a media blitz, queues down the street and great word of mouth. For three consecutive months, Colombo Social was the most googled restaurant in the country. Shaun said, 'It was insanity. You couldn't have scripted what happened.' Not only was the restaurant meeting the financial expectations that the loan officer had laughed at, but they were being doubled. Shaun paid his dad back, then he paid off some of his parents' debt and started saving for another venue.

It was the braveness of Shaun's career pivot that initially drew me to him – I'd seen him on *Australian Story* and knew I wanted to speak with him. He'd had a stable job, a good pathway forward, a goal he'd been working towards for so many years and a future all laid out. He hadn't been backed into a corner when he decided to do a full one-eighty. He'd just realised one day that he didn't want to spend the rest of his life on a path he wasn't passionate about. I don't know if I would be brave enough to do that.

For a few months, everything looked perfect. Then, in March 2020, COVID cases began to be reported in Australia and, like all Sydney restaurants, Colombo Social was forced to close.

\*

I first travelled to Sri Lanka in 2012, and I would return ten years later, immediately after the first Australian senior cricket tour of Pakistan in almost twenty-five years. Mark Taylor had captained the last time, in 1998, and in the second Test equalled Don Bradman's record of 334 runs in an innings. Three years after Taylor's tour, the 9/11 attacks happened in the United States. The war in Afghanistan began, Pakistan's western border became lawless and overrun with militants, and a period of terrorism started in Pakistan. An Australian tour of the country was planned in 2002, but that was moved to a neutral site after a suicide bomb attack was executed in a truck against a hotel close to where the New Zealand cricket team was staying.

Some international teams kept touring Pakistan until 2009, when the Indian team refused to play in Pakistan after terrorist attacks in Mumbai in November 2008. They were replaced by the Sri Lankan team, which was attacked by twelve terrorists as the players travelled to play at a stadium in Lahore. Seven of the Sri Lankans, including their captain, Mahela Jayawardene, were injured; a Pakistani umpire was shot twice in the chest; and two bystanders and six Pakistani policemen were killed.

More than a decade after that attack, an Australian delegation went to Pakistan to assess the security situation, and it was decided we could travel to Pakistan and play a three-Test series as well as ODI and T20 matches. There was some trepidation around the team, and I told the guys that if anyone didn't want to tour, we'd all fully understand their decision to stay home. But after the security protocols and risk assessments were explained, we fielded a full squad.

That tour was certainly one of the most eerie experiences I've had in cricket. We toured from hotel to stadium in bomb-proof buses on completely cleared streets, with military helicopters buzzing over the top of us and electronic countermeasures rendering every mobile phone in the area inert. The matches went off without hitch, though. The Pakistani players are no different to us, nor are the fans different to Australian fans – they love the game, they appreciate good play, and they seemed grateful that we'd come to their country to tour. Then we moved on to Sri Lanka, where we expected little drama but found it in spades.

Sri Lanka was in the middle of a severe economic crisis, with inflation, blackouts, and a shortage of fuel and gas. People were protesting out in the streets and, eventually, calling for the government to be sacked.

As a player, you're often oblivious to what's happening outside your hotel and off the pitch, but there were times that the crisis was obvious. One such instance was during the Test in the southern city of Galle. As we were playing, we could hear noises outside the stadium, and protesters could be seen from the Galle Fort overlooking the stadium. I didn't know it then, but now I know that this was a spontaneous protest after a group of people had tried to get gas bottles filled but were told there wasn't any gas. My team-mates and I didn't think that much about it until we heard sharp cracks coming from the hubbub outside.

I went over to the umpire, Kumar Dharmasena, to ask him what he thought was happening. 'Gunshots?' I asked.

'No.' He smiled. 'Just firecrackers.'

After that day's play, I went online to learn a bit more about what was going on, but there was only so much I could understand. I knew that the protesters were being supported by a number of current and former Sri Lankan players, including Kumar Sangakkara, Mahela Jayawardene and Muttiah Muralitharan. I asked a few of the Sri Lankan players whether it was a good thing that we were touring now, and they all said it was. The people appreciated that we were there, bringing excitement and tourism, and stimulating the economy.

At the end of the tour, my team-mates and I decided to donate our prize money to UNICEF, the organisation that was working in Sri Lanka to help kids and families impacted by the economic crisis, and also supports the Indi Kindi program.

*

In April 2020, the NSW and federal governments announced a series of initiatives that would keep businesses afloat and staff solvent during the COVID pandemic. The most significant of the federal initiatives was the JobKeeper wage subsidy, available to nearly all Australians. But it wasn't available to many of Shaun's staff, as people who held temporary visas – including refugees and asylum seekers – were not eligible.

'These people had become family,' said Shaun. 'I hated the idea that they were going to be left out. They'd been open with me, telling me their stories, and some had gone through hell and back and then built this great life with good work and a wage, and it was all going to stop?' He told me his concerns extended beyond the financial: he also didn't want his staff becoming sick. 'I just wanted them to be able to stay at home. I called every staff member and said, "I'm going to trust you a lot during this time. Text me how much it costs you per week to live … rent, food, everything."' He said everyone sent numbers that were excessively reasonable, and every week that amount of money went into their accounts.

To Shaun, looking after his staff was job one when the restaurant closed – job two was getting rid of the perishable food in Colombo Social's kitchen. 'We were like, "Let's put this stuff in containers and get it out the door."' With the help of a contact at Mission Australia's Common Ground project in Camperdown, and another at the Aboriginal Medical

Service Redfern, Shaun and his chefs got two hundred meals out the door in a couple of days.

Of course, the need didn't end there, though neither did Colombo Social's capacity to keep preparing food. In three weeks, the restaurant had taken on a number of charity partners as well as taking in international kitchen staff from other Sydney kitchens, including some notable chefs from hatted restaurants. 'We got to know the people we were feeding, and I think we helped a lot of lonely people,' said Shaun. He told me he became known, too, among the inner-city Sydney communities that the kitchen was feeding. 'No one knows my name, but there was a lot of, "You're the dude. You're that guy."' There was considerable appreciation from the community, because the staff were not only creating free meals, but they also cared about what they were cooking. 'Those meals were fucking delicious,' Shaun added.

Then, after three months of paying front-of-house staff and running a charity kitchen, the business could see the edge of a financial cliff approaching. 'We were running an efficient kitchen, but costs were just so high. Food and transport was through the roof.' Eventually the restaurant managed to turn away from the precipice when it opened again to customers and when Shaun and his business partner changed the business model. Colombo Social would become a social enterprise business, trading in a financially sustainable way but driven by a social purpose.

During the pandemic, the business was doing work that was simply charity, so Shaun and his business partner restructured it and its accounting accordingly, to a hybrid model, with both types of organisation working side by side under the new name Plate It Forward. The charity aspect of the business grew during and after COVID. From its start, donating 200 meals from perishable food that needed to be used, Plate It Forward has now donated 570,000 meals – 430,000 in Australia and the rest overseas.

It hasn't only been a story of providing food, either. Plate It Forward has provided vocational pathways for a lot of the people who have eaten its charity meals. These people now manage kitchens for homeless shelters and also run hospitality courses in a youth detention centre. Shaun's hiring policy expanded from asylum seekers to people who may have difficulty entering or re-entering the workforce, including former drug addicts, people from incarceration, and women escaping domestic violence or abuse. What came across to me about Shaun is that he sees the best in other people. He gives them an opportunity and responsibility and his trust in them is repaid.

In our interview, Shaun estimated that Plate It Forward had hired close to 200 people who would otherwise have had to rely on benefits. He said another of the stats he's most proud of is the ninety-seven per cent employment retention rate, which suggests these people love the security and sense of purpose the enterprise has given them.

In some ways, this sense of community that Shaun had established in Colombo Social reminded me of community cricket. Most of my cricketing life is playing professionally, but I spent my first 18-odd-years playing community cricket. These clubs are amazing places, not just because they give a start to people like me, but because they bring together so many different people who make them function, from coaches to people in charge of uniforms, to treasurers and people working in the canteen. It's never just the group walking out onto the field, it's also the parents and community behind and surrounding them. Each team or club has its own community within it, and that community extends beyond the game.

My home team is Penrith, and you get a real diverse set of people at different stages of their life there. It's a real 'put your arm around people' mentality too, as the cricket club becomes a touchpoint for a lot of people, and a place to ground them when other things going on in their life get tough. I'm sure for a lot of people the reason they keep coming back to the club isn't the on-field performances, but the support of their community and the direction and purpose it gives them. And it might be a bit of an escape from the real world too. Most clubs have off-season training groups nowadays too. Of course these are good to keep up fitness, but they also maintain the community touchpoints throughout the winter season when cricket isn't being played.

Shaun's goal was to make his customers happy, his employees safe, and to donate back to the communities abroad. I love win-wins like this, where it's not a zero-sum game. Everyone wins.

Colombo Social came back with a vengeance after lockdowns ended, and it has since spawned siblings. In the south-west fringe of Sydney's CBD, Shaun's team has opened a restaurant called Kyïv Social and, in the CBD, a restaurant called Kabul Social. Those restaurants hire Ukrainian and Afghan asylum seekers respectively, and they fund meals for those in need in Ukraine and Afghanistan.

So, what's next for Shaun? More, of course – more free meals, and more staff who might not be employed otherwise. There are more venues planned too. Shaun wants to open a restaurant in which he partners with Rohingya people escaping violence in Myanmar, and he has made an offer to partner with one of his Palestinian chefs, who lost a large number of family members to Israeli bombing in Gaza, in opening Gaza Social.

Shaun and his team are also about to partner with an Indigenous social enterprise in a venue in Redfern. That venue will use Indigenous-sourced, Australian native herbs and berries in all its meals, and exclusively hire Indigenous women. It will also be 'a bit more grab and go', according to Shaun. Furthermore, for every hundred meals sold, they will – through Adam Goodes, Michael O'Loughlin and James Gallichan's GO Foundation – give an Indigenous kid a scholarship to go through school for a year. 'Uber are going to match that too,' said Shaun, 'so it'll be two scholarships every hundred meals.'

Another project Shaun's working on at the moment is opening a kitchen in Batticaloa, where his mum was born. At this kitchen, women over the age of seventy who don't have livelihoods and were affected by the civil war will cook food from his mother's recipes, and that food will be donated around the city. Shaun plans to have the kitchen open for his mum's seventieth birthday next year: it will be her present. He said he feels as though he owes his mum, not only for the things she did for him growing up, but also for instilling in him a desire to help others – which, he told me, has kept him out of a life that was lucrative but potentially miserable.

Shaun lives a life he says feels forever unfinished; after all, the meals he donates will never be able to fill all the empty stomachs in Sydney's urban centre, let alone in Sri Lanka, Afghanistan or Ukraine, and there will always be people who've been left out of the labour market. However, he now lives a life that he says has him energetically bounding out of bed in the morning, ready to do more good work. Even if sometimes that's at 10 am – he is in hospitality, after all.

'It was Mum who pushed me to do all this, who pushed all of us to do our stuff,' Shaun said, referring to the fact that his brothers, both of whom were also in finance, now also work for not-for-profit or socially responsible companies. 'It's what Mum did, telling us to think about the world differently. Give back, do something. It was her.' Shaun added, 'Trust me. It wasn't us. Me and my brothers are not that fucking good.'

I'm not so sure she can take all the credit, though. An interesting thread I found while working on this book is that so many people who are tested in their lives are left with an inclination to give back.

\*

My mum always used to tell us kids to consider the lives of people we didn't know. She first started saying this when we were little, after me or my brothers and sisters said something offhand about another kid or someone struggling out in the neighbourhood. Mum didn't like that. She'd tell us off, saying that we didn't know anything about those people's lives, backgrounds or circumstances. She'd tell us that every person is trying and has a story and a role in the world, even if we couldn't understand it. Then she'd remind us how lucky we were. She'd always say that: we were lucky. 'Okay, Mum, yep, I'm lucky,' I'd say. I didn't feel any luckier than anyone else I knew.

She kept telling us that we were lucky when we were older too, adding that we had to do something with our luck. She told us we'd had a head start in life, and we had to do something with it. She wanted us to live good lives – caring lives of achievement. She lived her principles too, volunteering in the neighbourhood and, one day a week, going out with a soup kitchen to feed people who were food-insecure.

I often didn't really understand what Mum meant when she said we were lucky. To me, our family seemed perfectly average in most respects.

Mum would tell us not to get caught up on money and cars and those sorts of things. She said we were lucky because we had each other, and that we were cared for and that our lives were our own, not dragged down. 'Got it, Mum.' Then I'd be off to school or training or whatever. I didn't actually think that much about the luck I'd been born into until

I was older – not when I started my immensely fortunate cricketing career, but more recently, when I started my own family.

I also thought about my luck more when my mum passed away. One of the sad ironies of the loss of someone you love is that you somehow get to consider their inner thoughts and feelings more than you had before. Also, it's hard to consider good luck without understanding the devastating and random nature of bad luck.

I was lucky and I am lucky. I know that now. Albie is lucky too, but of course he doesn't know it yet.

I've been learning a bit recently about how empathy works in kids. As I write this, my son is turning three, so around now he's developing a capacity psychologists call 'theory of mind'. This explains the dawning realisation in little kids that other people's emotions and thoughts may be different to theirs. It's an interesting phenomenon, seemingly tied to a child's rising language capabilities and their interest in stories.

One day a toddler will have no response to the injury or sadness of other people, except perhaps annoyance and frustration, and the next they'll start to be concerned and perhaps even put a hand on the other person and ask if they're okay. This change is because the kids have developed an ability to build a model of what that moment may feel like for the other person. It's essentially, in their mind, an understanding of the other person's mind, a skill honed by being around other people with other desires and difficulties, and by reading or learning about characters overcoming and struggling, and succeeding and failing. If another person is feeling pain or sadness, the child can for the first time feel some of that pain and sadness too. Sometimes that shared feeling might result in an action, like a hug or the sharing of a toy.

This is where everybody's lifelong journey of empathy and compassion begins. Where that journey ends and what course it takes, however, is different for everyone. Most of us feel compassion and empathy for our families, and perhaps for our neighbours, co-workers and friends, but what about others in our neighbourhood or city? What about people in other cities and other countries? Each of us has to figure that out for ourself, usually with a bit of guidance along the way. I hope to guide my children in their journey in the years to come. Mum guided me on mine, and does still, as Shaun's mum does on his journey and forever will.

# 7

## Don't ask for an easy life: you want to be able to thrive in a hard one

*A conversation with Nedd Brockmann*

I GREW UP AT THE FOOT OF THE BLUE MOUNTAINS, with the bush on our doorstep, the CBD a world away and the watering holes of Glenbrook National Park our main relief on hot summer days. These days I live in Sydney's eastern suburbs, between the ocean and the city, only a short drive from the SCG. It's a long way from home, in a lot of ways. It's flashier than the west, and more hectic, but it is a really beautiful spot. As much as I love the beaches – especially the one we're a strong outfield throw away from – my favourite thing about the area is the mix of people. There are establishment types and families who've lived there for generations, but mostly I mix with a younger group who have come to Sydney's east from across the country and the world, full of plans and aspirations. I guess I fit into that category myself.

My mates, who I meet at the pub sometimes for a schnitzel and trivia, share stories about their lives, but they also plan. That's one of the things I like about our group:

everyone's moving and everyone's planning. One of these mates is a guy called Nedd Brockmann, a former sparky and now professional runner with a shock of white-blond hair that sticks out the back of his hat when he's running, which is pretty much always. Rain, hail or shine, you can see him pounding the pavement around Sydney's east and especially around Centennial Park. Our age difference is only five years, but I often feel that there's a generational divide somewhere in there. In Nedd, however, I've found a parity of spirit – I love his energy and I always come away pumped whenever we catch up. There's a boldness and a relentlessness to the bloke that's pretty enthralling, and that is in me sometimes too.

Nedd's built a name for himself raising millions of dollars for charity, raising awareness of homelessness and in the process raising awareness of himself. He's become an inspiration to many people, including me. How's he done all that? By running, basically. But more than that, he's done it by enduring pain, blisters, shin splints and doubt. Nedd Brockmann has a skill, and that skill is an inability to quit. Unlike so many of the people in this book, whose moments of being tested happened to them whether they wanted it or not, Nedd went and sought out that testing moment, to push himself, to discover his limits and so discover something about himself.

If you already know about Nedd, then that's probably from the run he did from Perth to Sydney in 2022. You may have followed him on his journey through Instagram and listened along as he posted his 'song of the day', but it's more likely than not that you first knew of him after the run. You probably saw images of him arriving at the end of it with his arms in the air as thousands of residents in Sydney's east celebrated a newly minted hero. Those photos were shared far and wide, on the news and on social media feeds across the world.

It's a moment that can be enjoyed at a glance – a young bloke achieving his dream of running the breadth of the country – but it can be enjoyed more deeply when you know something of Nedd's history, motivation, personality and drive. Even understanding his choice of destination for his big run brings a little bit more drama and meaning to the image of him spraying Champagne over a giant crowd at Bondi Surf Bathers' Life Saving Club. It did for me, anyway.

I had always assumed that Nedd ended the run at Bondi because it's an iconic beach, a place his sponsors and media partners preferred, but it turns out the destination was Nedd's preference. In his mind, Sydney's east was a place of oversized significance. For the boy who grew up on a cattle farm, Bondi Beach was a place where people fully fulfilled life's promise; where they had fit bodies, wore stylish clothes and had money in their pockets. Even when Nedd moved to Sydney to study at TAFE, living just up the road from Bondi and going there often enough to see that its shimmer and sheen doesn't always match the reality of the place, the idea of Bondi loomed large in his consciousness.

When Nedd had the idea of conducting his big run, there was no other place he could run to than Bondi. In running there, he was racing to glory, and he told me he thought he was also running symbolically towards the life he'd always wanted. Along the way, however, he found a place that was even more desirable, attractive and seductive than Bondi at its shimmering best.

*

Nedd Brockmann grew up just outside of Forbes, five hours west of Sydney. His mum, Kylie, worked as an accountant and personal trainer, while his dad, Ian, ran the family cattle farm. Nedd said some of his first and most enduring memories are of his dad doing that work, up well before the sun to tend to the cattle and then home to help tend to Nedd and his brother and sister, Logan and Mabel.

Nedd said he can't exactly identify where his own drive and fire emerged, but if he had to attribute it to something, he'd probably point to his dad and the example he set when Nedd was a boy. 'Dad wasn't just given everything, but he built a life for all of us. He just went out there and did it, and he showed us how. He showed that you had to sacrifice to have anything, and that you had to work your arse off, and he did it because he had three kids. I didn't know exactly how much he was sacrificing, but I was watching that as a kid and learning. I was learning how to be a stoic.'

Nedd went to a local primary school attended by only two dozen kids, before moving to Kinross Wolaroi School in Orange. In that school, he said, he was just another kid in a population of thousands. He added that in this period of anonymity, a desire grew in him to be great at something – anything.

He told me he was a pretty good athlete and undoubtedly more accomplished in sport than academics, so he assumed if he worked exceptionally hard in his sporting endeavours, that was where he'd eventually stand out. Like most of the boys at the school, he played rugby union. On the pitch he found himself a pretty decent if undersized player. He wasn't a player that Super Rugby clubs were ever going to be throwing contracts at, though.

Nedd rowed too. On the creek where his team trained he was better as a rower than he was on the pitch as a rugby player, but even in the boat he was merely good. 'I was just never great at stuff. I was never bad, but I was never succeeding the way I wanted to. I worked hard, but I was never like the best at anything. I trained my arse off rowing, and I'd do fourteen different races in one day and at the end wouldn't podium in any of them. I'd always get off the boat and just like lay down and think, *When is this going to happen?* I remember saying it to Mum once, and she told me just to slow down and not to worry: "Just don't let it defeat you. It will come."' He might not place, but he was always the guy who would finish – usually vomiting because he'd given it absolutely everything.

Time rolled on. Nedd left school, and the workforce beckoned. As a young man of ambition and drive, he wanted to try life in the big city, so he moved to Sydney and started an apprenticeship that required study at TAFE NSW Ultimo in the CBD. He soon saw the best and worst of the big city. He met people who were making money and fulfilling their dreams, and he also saw people who seemed to have been forgotten. He was confronted with the issue of homelessness, which was far more visible in Sydney than in Forbes or Orange.

Nedd, then just out of his teens, was wondering what his life might be like. He was studying to be an electrician, and with that valuable skill he might be able to own a small business one day, but could he have more? Nedd told me that he felt in his belly that there was something else for him – something big.

For a time, according to Nedd, he became caught up in all the big city can offer to any young guy with a job and a bit of money in his pocket. Nedd was living differently to the people back home, but not that differently to everyone else in the city. He drank a little too much, ate the wrong foods and put some weight on. Then he began running: 'I just started running to lose weight, and then I ran a bit further and a bit further, and I was like, *Fuck, I wonder how far I could take this.*'

'How far' became a significant thought. Nedd was a pretty fast middle-distance and long-distance runner, but he wasn't setting himself apart from the rest of the world with his pace. He found that when he ran, he could keep going, day after day. It wasn't that he didn't feel the pain and exhaustion of such a run, it was just that he could feel this discomfort and go on anyway. He told me, 'It's not that I love running. I don't really like it at all. It's just the one thing I know I can do and I'm quite good at. Yeah. So let's do it! Yeah. And that just kind of became my thing.'

Nedd started running every day and eventually decided he wanted to test himself. He said he could have run a marathon, but in his eyes, what was the point? He ran forty-two kilometres regularly. He probably would have managed a decent time in a competitive marathon, but he wasn't going to win any major marathons: he was just going to be another runner, his time just another time. He wanted a unique challenge, but one that would still allow him to go to work for eight hours, five days a week. He wanted to do something hard – that was the point of the thing. He wanted to do something that was so hard, people would hear about it and wonder whether it was even possible.

On 24 July 2020, Nedd finished work and ran for the next eight and a half hours, from Randwick to Palm Beach and back – a distance of 103 kilometres, the furthest he'd ever run in one day. After he posted about it on his Instagram account, which had a couple of thousand followers, a smattering of congratulatory comments and messages came in.

Three days after his hundred-kilometre run, Nedd posted a message on Instagram that started with: 'PLEASE READ!!' It went on to say that from 31 August, he would run fifty consecutive marathon-distance runs for fifty days, with each run beginning at 4 pm, right after work. He would run fifty consecutive marathons – *would*, not might, not may. He didn't plan to run fifty marathons: he would.

Nedd told me that this moment of commitment, when he says he'll do something, is huge for him. Ideas are cheap, he said, but from the moment you say you'll do something, you can start to learn a lot about yourself. In every difficult endeavour there are moments when it would make sense to back out; he reckons the difference between him and most people is that he never will and never could. 'Everyone's had an idea, everyone has something they're going to do that's special, but who does it? If I say I'm going to do something out loud, that's it. I have to do it.'

The marathons were to be a mix of laps at Centennial Park in Sydney's east, treadmill turns at a gym close to his house, and street runs to mix things up a bit. Without any organised help, he started promoting himself on his social media feed. He set up a fundraising link where he asked people who were inspired by what he was doing to donate; the money would go to Red Cross.

On the eve of his first run, and after a bit of local media coverage about this mad sparky's plan to run himself ragged after work every day, Nedd had managed to get about $12,000 worth of pledges to Red Cross. Then, on Monday, 31 August, he started running. The first marathon was trotted on the flat track that is the Centennial Park loop. He posted the details of the run, which had him doing five-and-a-half-minute kilometres for a total time of just under four hours. At the bottom of the post was an idiom that would become a mantra for Nedd: 'Get comfortable being uncomfortable.'

The posts were uploaded on days two, three, four – and every day until days twenty, thirty and forty. All of the posts dripped with sweaty enthusiasm. Some announced sponsors who'd jumped on board, some updated the fundraising total, some had quotes of the day or songs of the day, which became a Nedd Brockmann hallmark later on, and all were signed off with: 'Get comfortable being uncomfortable.'

As he ran, Nedd got faster, finishing the fiftieth and final marathon – again a Centennial Park loop – more than an hour quicker than the first, which gave him his first time under three hours. At the end of that marathon, the national media came on board, offering Nedd a spot on the *Today Show*. The $12,000 pledge to the Red Cross ballooned out past $100,000.

Only at the end of the day that Nedd described to me 'as the best day of my life' did he admit to anyone just how painful the last few marathons had been. He'd sustained serious injuries to his toes, an Achilles strain, and soft-tissue injuries to his calves, hamstrings and quads, and he'd needed treatment to his femurs and hips also. He hadn't missed any of the fifty runs, however; he'd said he was going to do fifty marathons in fifty days, so that was what he had done.

After recovering, Nedd kept running and kept posting. Some runs were short and some were long, including one in which he decided to attack the 440, a running loop at Bronte Beach that incorporates a steep incline. He wouldn't run it the ten times that locals do every Saturday morning, but 200 times, for a total distance of 143 kilometres, at a total elevation of 5000 metres. And this was just an everyday run.

In some ways, the way Nedd was pushing himself is a lot like the conditioning sessions we'll do in cricket pre-season. We push ourselves as hard as we can so that we learn our limits, and also so that when we're playing in a game it all seems easy. The important thing is, we do it all in a controlled session and with safety parameters so that if we fail at least there's someone there to catch us, and enough time to recover before the real challenge hits.

I like pushing myself like this, knowing that I'll be okay, but Nedd is the opposite – he's scared of the goals he sets himself, and he's never a hundred per cent sure he's going to be okay on the other side. But for him, that's the challenge.

In each of Nedd's new posts was his endless enthusiasm and vigour, and his ongoing exhortation that everyone needs to be comfortable being uncomfortable. Knowing Nedd as I do, all of this came from a place of real truth – he's exactly the same person in public as he is in real life. None of the challenges he set himself were for the public persona alone, if he says he's going to have cold showers for six months to see what it's like, he's doing it because he genuinely wants to know. In this authenticity, his social media presence grew, and more messages came from the public, asking, 'What next?'

Nedd had something in mind. The next big run had to be bigger, longer and more difficult. He reckoned this was the thing, this was what his life was all about. He wanted to make a splash, and he wanted to change his life. He'd have to do something that people would notice, and not just the people who had noticed his after-work marathons. It also had to be something that was possible. After all, as far as he was concerned, the worst fate in the world was saying he was going to do something, then quitting.

In April 2022, Nedd made his announcement, not only on Instagram but also on the *Today Show*. He was going to fly to Perth and run four thousand kilometres east until he hit the beach, and he was going to do it in forty days. That meant he was going to run a hundred kilometres every day for nearly six weeks.

'I wasn't prepared for that run at all,' Nedd told me with a laugh.

\*

On 1 September 2022, amid a small crowd of well-wishers, Nedd started running away from Cottesloe Beach. First he left Perth, then the Western Australian wheatbelt, then the goldfields, and then he ran on towards the edge of the Nullarbor Plain.

Only a few days into the run, Nedd started to understand the immense difficulty of the task he'd set himself. The pain was commensurate to what he'd felt during his latter marathons, and then there was more pain and more again. His hips, back and legs were in pain, but usually the worst was in his ankles, one of which became so swollen that he couldn't move his toes or foot. After each day, when he took his shoes off and started to try to get some rest, it was as though he and his support crew were playing Whac-A-Mole, treating one issue as another was getting ready to flare up.

'It was a bit of a cowboy operation,' said Nedd. 'But the one thing I did have on my side was that there was no possible way I wasn't getting to Bondi. Every time I had to make a decision, it had to get me closer to Bondi. If [the decisions] weren't going to do that, then we had to come up with something else. Easy.'

Just shy of the border between Western Australia and South Australia, Nedd jumped on a Zoom call with a doctor and then was driven 14 hours to the nearest MRI machine, in Whyalla, for a scan of his ankles and feet. The doctor ordered that he stop running for at least six weeks. With that suggestion a non-starter, Nedd asked if there was anything else he could do. There wasn't, the doctor told him, but cortisone injections might help with the pain. So Nedd had the cortisone injections in Whyalla, was driven 14 hours back to the border and kept running.

The ankle issue persisted and continued to contribute to issues with his feet. Pus developed in his toes, and every day became a battle between Nedd and his foot injuries. The consistent pain meant he was barely sleeping. 'I was completely delirious,' he said.

The mornings were the worst and the best part of his day. He'd wake up in significant amounts of pain, usually having had fewer than three or four hours of continuous sleep. These moments, Nedd told me, were when he had to recommit to himself and his run. He added that while his running training regimen was 'a bit amateurish', he'd prepared for these moments of shaking himself into a state of consciousness and hitting the road. For a year before the big run, he had set his alarm for 4 am, regardless of what had happened the day before. Whatever happened, no matter how he felt, he told himself he would get up and run. So he did, every time, in the lead-up to his run across Australia and while he was completing it.

Nedd said that once he was up and running in the morning, there was no quit in him until the next morning before he set off. No matter how hard things got, or how painful, the only option was forward. No matter how bad Nedd's body got, the pain of having said he'd do something and then not doing it was always going to be the greater agony. So he kept going.

A phrase emerged in Nedd's head during those long, painful days: Showing up. 'I kept wondering, *Can I show up?* I was asking, *Will I be a man of my word?* I wanted to be, so I was.' Nedd told me that this decision made things far easier for him. When the run became about showing up, any answer to any problem became acceptable – except quitting. 'It was like, someone throws you two kilometres out in the ocean and you have to get home, yeah. What are you gonna do? You gonna drown? Are you gonna get home? It's like a kid learning to run. It's hard, but what are you going to do? Stop? Never. Never.'

Nedd said sometimes the only option available to him, when the injuries and pain were immense, was to bend reality. 'In that moment of *How am I going to keep going?* there was usually so much out of my control, but the one thing I could always do is say how fucking good I felt. At times I couldn't even take another step without agony, but in those moments I would say how good I felt and then laugh and take another step.' He said that when he was in searing pain and feeling delirious with fatigue while telling himself he felt 'fucking good', he wasn't lying to himself. He wanted greatness in his life, and he wanted excellence, and here it was for the taking.

When Nedd was rowing, he just wasn't fast enough. No matter how hard he trained, no matter how deep he dug, he was never going to be fast enough. When he played rugby, he wasn't big or skilled enough – and he could never change that. All Nedd Brockmann wanted as a kid was a chance to become great and to find the thing that set him apart. And here it was.

'I think that's the purest moment,' he told me. 'It's like you're just ... you're so in it. You've made this thing up for yourself, like you've chosen to do this thing. Everyone's around it. People put money into it. People put time and energy into it, and you're there and it's on you to get this done. So off you go.'

Off he went. Back on the road, with his pain, his fatigue and his chance to be different to everybody else. 'Best time of my life,' said Nedd.

*

I debuted in the Australian Test side in 2011, but I wasn't really part of it until 2017, thanks to a long period in which I struggled to get my body right to be able to have the stresses of Test cricket put on it. After playing a couple of Tests in India in 2017, I flew over to Bangladesh for what was one of the most memorable Tests of my career.

Before we even stepped on the pitch, there was drama hanging over everything. In the lead-up to the event, a pay dispute had threatened to scuttle the series. There were also serious security concerns beyond any I'd heard of before, as the county had suffered a series of terrorist attacks; for that series we had a level of security that is usually reserved for a visiting head of state, some of which is seen but most of which is felt.

Then, as we started training and getting acclimatised, none of us were thinking about pay or even security concerns – it was impossible to think about anything except the relentless heat and humidity that blanketed the country, day and night. Before even playing a Test in the series, Glenn Maxwell had to be treated by the team doctor for heatstroke, then Peter Handscomb succumbed also. It was like nothing I've felt before or since: it was all-encompassing. Every step was a chore, let alone running in and bowling.

I had difficulty that series. I was a junior quick and expected to get good, hard overs in, but I couldn't get at the Bangladeshis. Beyond the demonic heat, I just couldn't get the ball to do anything for me and couldn't chip away at their defences. I charged in and charged in and charged in, working my arse off for very little return – and yet I'll always remember that Test series fondly.

I've always enjoyed being in the middle of a physical contest where everyone is hurting. I also appreciate that it's only in those moments, when you're up against it, that you can find out what you're made of. When you're sitting on the couch at home, or you're at training, or you're a little bloke dreaming of great moments, you can tell yourself there's nothing you won't do to get to your goal, but you actually have no idea – not until you're there, at the precipice of what's possible.

When I was a boy, I had fantasized about the type of situation I was in during that Test in Bangladesh. I'd be in the backyard, facing down one of my older brothers, and in my mind, a Test would be in the balance, my spot in the side at risk, the conditions would be abhorrent, the situation dire, and I'd just needed to keep going, and to keep fighting, keep bowling. In those moments, it wouldn't be about winning anymore. I wanted to be the guy who stood up, went hardest for longest, and was willing to push myself further than anyone else on the field. I would tell myself, *I just need to ignore my aching body and bowl one more good ball. I can do it. I can do it.* I'd relish those moments.

Maybe it was the little brother in me, trying to keep up with my older, stronger brothers.

In Bangladesh, that mindset was tested for real. Did I have another over in me? How badly did I want it? What a thrill. What a moment. What a privilege. Moments of absolute difficulty like that always make me want to go harder and longer, and to see who I really am among other professionals. This is the essence of Test cricket.

This appreciation for the difficult is the place where Nedd and I meet. It's why we're friends and why I wanted to speak to him for this book. In both Nedd and me is a raging spirit of competition. He's a thoughtful and considerate person, and I like to think I am too, but I reckon both of us have a mongrel in us, one that is woken when we start competing. When there are only two options available, pain or submission, both of us will choose pain every single time, because we see submission as the true pain. In the wrong context, aggression, combativeness and stubbornness can be toxic, undoubtedly. However, in the context of sport, exploration and endeavour, they can be necessary.

We live in a very different world to the one where the fast bowlers of the seventies lived. It's not appropriate for me to play or live exactly how they did – but to play well, I need the dog in me sometimes. I need to stare down the pitch the way they did, with the same fire in my chest that they had. To play well, I need to want to be the best.

A heightened sense of competitiveness can get a bad rap sometimes, but I tell you, when you're in the last few overs of a fruitless and overheated spell, in a Test that not that many people are watching back home, or if you're out running on the seemingly endless Nullarbor with only your weeping blisters to keep you company, it can be a hell of a drug.

\*

If Nedd achieved his goal of getting from Cottesloe to Bondi in forty days, he'd be the fastest bloke to run across the country and would fulfil his dream of living his life to its fullest. But it was in the first seven days of running that he realised he wasn't going to get to Bondi in forty days, not with his feet and ankles the way they were. The realisation wasn't a depressing one, however: it was liberating and enlightening. Getting there first and fastest just wasn't what he was all about – it never had been. Fastest wasn't what he was best at. First wasn't his calling. Nedd was about something else altogether.

Nedd Brockmann was about showing up. His talent wasn't to get the glittering prize after he jostled with competitors in a packed stadium; his talent was to show up and do the work, regardless of the circumstances. Nedd realised he was never about chasing anyone else's heels, he was about showing up. Then showing up, showing up and showing up, alone, in the dark, likely in pain and with an endless horizon ahead of him. Nedd did just that throughout the second week of running – and the third, fourth, fifth, sixth and seventh.

Media and social interest grew and then grew again. As Nedd ran through the eastern part of New South Wales and towards Sydney's outskirts, people on social media shared his posts in a contagious wave. As he ran through Sydney's east, a huge crowd gathered in Bondi. And when he finally ran down the hill approaching Bondi, hundreds cheered from the roadside and from bars, cafés and restaurants. On the boardwalk above Bondi Beach, where Nedd was going to finish his run, ten thousand people packed themselves in to cheer his final steps. He crossed the line in a scene that could have finished a Hollywood film, with a bank of photographers and TV cameras capturing him being carried aloft by the crowd as he drank Champagne in front of one of Australia's most perfect beaches.

Nedd had done what he'd said he would do, and he had captured the imagination of a hell of a lot of people. Like Dennis Lillee, he'd taken charge of the direction of his life, and wouldn't take no for an answer. He'd changed his own life forever, but not only his. Through his run across the country, he raised money for We Are Mobilise, a charity that addresses the root causes of homelessness and helps make transformational change. It's a charity he continues to work with, pledging money but also spearheading a message that homelessness should not equal hopelessness. His run raised $2.6 million, which would give a lot of people the tools to pull themselves out of homelessness.

Was that Bondi afternoon, when he arrived like a conquering hero, to crowds and accolades, Nedd's greatest moment? He told me, 'It was a great moment, don't get me wrong. It's not what I'll remember best, though.'

What Nedd remembered most fondly about the run were the moments when he was alone on the side of the road, knowing for sure that he was going to stop, but then he'd kept going. Moments when, suffering from chafing, blistering and fatigue, he'd told himself he was having the best time of his life – and believed it. He said those are the moments he cherishes and also the ones that nourish him. The writer Ernest Hemingway reflected on his youth as a 'moveable feast' from which he could eat for the rest of his life. In the same way, Nedd's incredibly hard times give him strength to this day. Circumstances can change easily, but mindset? That endures.

*

Nedd said he didn't consciously plan for running to change his life. Unconsciously, however, this may have been the plan all along. 'Mum reminded me [after my big run] of this diary I had, and it had this five-year plan. I got chills when I opened it up. It said, *You're going to do running to make money so you don't have to work as a sparky.*'

Now Nedd's running means he doesn't have to work as a sparky. He has written a bestselling book, which is a great read that I recommend to everyone, and he's even launched his own choccy milk, Nedd's Milk. Both ventures also benefit charity. Beyond that, he has corporate sponsorships and is also pretty popular on the speaking circuit. In many ways, he told me, he lives his life now in the spirit of those great adventurers and explorers who have come before him. It's not to hear about the Nullarbor Plain that anybody books Nedd for a speaking engagement or reads his book, *Showing Up*: they want to know what it's like inside the big mental holes he found himself in during his big run, and how he got out again.

When I suggested to Nedd that he is comparable to motivational public figures like Wim Hof, David Goggins and Rich Roll – who are all about finding another way to live a modern life, forgoing some conveniences in order to access a satisfaction that can only be earned through discipline, physical fitness and extremely hard work – Nedd vehemently agreed. 'Some people want absolute comfort, and it's easy to live comfortably today. A phone is all you need to get your food delivered. For so many of us, life is so easy now. We're so removed from what we were ten thousand years ago. We're not meant to just swipe and scroll.'

He told me that the thing people most commonly say to him after his speaking engagements is that they're considering leaving their jobs, and he told me that's not his message at all. 'I tell people, "It's not for everyone." Some people just want security and enjoyment; their fulfilment is reading or family or whatever. That's the coolest thing for them. For me it's one thing, for you it might be sitting and reading. The point is not that you need to do something extreme – the point is that you will do things that you're supposed to be doing.'

Nedd says showing up can mean different things to different people. For him, right now, showing up means, for better or worse, tests of extreme endurance – even though they might seem unreasonable, over the top or even just plain dangerous to his health. For others, showing up might mean applying themselves completely to their family, jobs or values. He says it's just about finding out what you want to do, saying that out loud and doing what you said you'd do. He cites his brother as a salaried family man who has found his bliss and is living it. This, Nedd told me, may end up being what 'showing up' is to him. 'I'm not living for a moment, I'm living for a movement. I don't want to just try to piggyback off this run and go, "Woohoo, I raised $2.6 million for charity." I want to evolve and keep evolving.'

For Nedd, who's still young, fit and full of athletic ambition, next he's going to run a thousand miles and will try to do it in less than ten days and ten hours, 30 minutes and 36 seconds, which is the fastest that distance has ever been run. He's also given himself a charity fundraising goal of $10 million.

By the time this book comes out, Nedd should have just finished his run. If he hasn't finished it, it won't be for lack of trying.

'I'm in a flow state even now, I reckon,' he said. 'And I'm already connected to some pretty awesome moments in the future I can't wait to get to. It's a pretty fascinating way to be.'

What's extraordinary is that Nedd didn't start out as a runner, and the amount of work he had to put in before that forty-day run is about ten years of work in two years of training. It'd be like me wanting to be one of the greatest endurance rowers in just two years, even though I'd rarely rowed before. To do the sorts of things Nedd has done takes drive and focus. For him, every waking minute is about getting to his next goal.

In some ways, this book is an experiment in discovering what's out there, where other people have had their limits pushed and returned to tell the tale. Part of the discovery process has been seeking out other people to learn from. Nedd, however, wants to learn from himself. He doesn't wait for things to happen to him, or rely on others to provide the answers he seeks; he challenges himself, pushes himself to the extreme in order to find those answers.

When something hits us, we often look elsewhere for answers. But what Nedd has taught me is the value of looking within as well.

# 8

## We can't succeed until we've learned how to fail, and we can't learn how to fail until we know ourselves

*A conversation with Elizabeth Day*

WHEN I STARTED INTERVIEWING PEOPLE FOR THIS book, I didn't realise how much we would end up talking about failure as much as success. The people I interviewed have all achieved extraordinary successes, but each of them has also failed numerous times along the way. What all of the people I spoke to share, however, is that none of them allowed their failures to define them. They instead used those failures as stepping stones to greater success. This may seem strange to say, but perhaps the one thing you really don't want to fail at is failure itself.

Elizabeth Day, a British writer, has a lot of fascinating things to say about failure. As the host of the podcast *How to Fail* and the author of a book of the same name, Elizabeth spends much of her professional life considering failure, both her own and that of others. She understands the mechanics of failure and has good tips on how to fail successfully – and in our interview, she had more to share with me than just that. She has considered the philosophical implications of failure, how it forces us to be humble and how, through our failures, we can learn to connect with the people around us.

When I spoke with Elizabeth for this book, it was over Zoom. We met again when I sat down with her in London to record an episode of her podcast. We spoke a lot about time management and life priorities, but also about the time I failed at being a farmer.

Becky and I have about twenty-five hectares and nine cattle on our property. I love it there – it's at such a different pace to 'normal' cricket life – and two days down at the farm feels like a two week break.

One time, I'd planted out a new garden full of flowering plants, including a row of gorgeous hydrangeas along the fence line. About a month later, we went down to find that the cows had reached over the fence and eaten all the hydrangeas, and what the cows hadn't eaten, the winter cold had killed!

I've already discussed in Nedd's chapter the benefit of conditioning training in the off-season – how we push ourselves until our bodies fail us in order to learn our limits, and do so in a safe and controlled environment where we can fail safely. For me, farming feels much the same. I'm not a successful farmer, but that's okay – I'm a novice at it, and the experience of failing privately, when there isn't anything big on the line, reminds me that there are still things I have to learn. I also like the experience of trying to master a new skill, and the joy in challenging myself to do so is one shared by many of the people in this book.

One of my neighbours told me, 'You might get the odd win against Mother Nature, but don't count on winning too much.' That's something else I like about farm life – you can control some things, but a lot of it is down to fortune.

A lot of people think of failure as the end of something, but the more you fail, the more you realise that there is a life after failure and that it only defines you if you let it.

*

Elizabeth Day may be best known for her extremely popular podcast, but she told me that writing and reading are the centre of her being. 'I understand the world through books,' she said.

As a child, she was bookish and curious – traits that have served her well as a writer – but she said she had other traits that weren't so useful. I wouldn't have known it, because she was speaking to me about things I'm not sure I'd ever spoken to a stranger about before, but Elizabeth said she grew up a very shy and reticent girl. She also said she was unable then to acknowledge her emotions.

As a girl she had been buttoned-down and pliant, and she credits that to two factors: time – she was born in 1978 – and place; at the time she was growing up, English people, and English girls especially, didn't bare their emotional lives, not in her middle-class family, anyway. And while she was an English girl and part of an English family, Elizabeth didn't grow up in England. She grew up in Northern Ireland during The Troubles, where loose chat wasn't just socially unacceptable but also dangerous, and where a famous saying emerged on the streets: 'If you have to say something, say nothing.'

Elizabeth and her family moved to Northern Ireland when Elizabeth was still an infant, so that her father could take up a residency at Altnagelvin Hospital in the contested city of Derry, working as a general surgeon. Throughout Elizabeth's childhood, The Troubles raged: the sectarian war between Irish Catholic nationalists, who believed Northern Ireland should be reunited with the rest of Ireland, and Protestant unionists, who believed Northern Ireland should stay part of the United Kingdom. While groups like the IRA didn't have much interest in English schoolgirls like Elizabeth, she decided it was wise to become someone who observed rather than interacted.

Elizabeth told me that in Northern Ireland, 'an English accent could tend to mark you at best as an outsider or, in some instances, an enemy, so in public I often just kept my mouth shut.' She became an 'observer of the human condition' and said she was always considering what other people were thinking and feeling. She added that this capacity for empathy was in contrast to her understanding of her own emotions, which were always suppressed – except in the case of one emotion. That emotion was desire, focused specifically into a desire to please authority figures.

'I was raised to be thoughtful and pliant and kind to others and nice,' said Elizabeth. 'That made me someone who tried very hard to please others.' She wanted to please her parents, she said, but she also wanted to please her teachers. '[That desire was] linked to my self-esteem. I always had low self-esteem, and I think pleasing others became a placeholder for self-esteem. I had low self-esteem, but at least I had high grades.'

After high school, Elizabeth left Northern Ireland to take up a spot offered at Queens' College, Cambridge, one of the most prestigious universities in the world. There her academic excellence continued: she graduated with a double first in History, meaning she obtained a first in both parts of her degree, a rare achievement at a place like Cambridge.

Elizabeth said she always had a writing career in mind. While studying at Cambridge and considering an application for a Masters in Journalism, she was hired by a London-based newspaper, *The Evening Standard*. There she worked under the legendary British non-fiction writer and historian Max Hastings as a diarist and social writer, and she quickly made a name for herself. In 2004 she was named the British Press Awards Young Journalist of the Year. Later she became a feature writer at *The Evening Standard*, a news reporter at *The Sunday Telegraph*, feature writer at *The Mail on Sunday* and then *The Observer*, where she worked with a wide remit.

At age twenty-nine, Elizabeth started dating a fellow journalist with a relatively high profile. His was a big name in British journalism, and he later became the editorial director of *BBC News*. The pair married in 2011, and Elizabeth told me, 'If you only knew me from a distance or if you knew me professionally, it looked like life was great.' Only it wasn't.

Elizabeth said she was unsettled in that period, adding that much of that unhappiness was because she thought primarily of others. 'I always thought the most important thing was to please people and to be kind. But kindness is a slightly different thing from people-pleasing. I was trying to figure out what I thought others wanted of me and then shapeshift according to projected desires, which is a terrible way to conduct any relationship as it proved.'

Elizabeth said her marriage was failing, but she couldn't admit that to herself. As a writer, Elizabeth was paid to understand the world around her, but she admits she still didn't understand herself well. There was an empty feeling inside that she couldn't escape.

'I felt like I was failing at conventional life because I was in my London life where at the time the biggest aspiration was a terraced house and two kids going to the same schools as everyone else's. I had such a specific plan for my life. I thought I'd be a journalist and writer and I'd get married and have children, and it was quite a conventional, heteronormative plan, and then, at age thirty-five, that plan imploded in quite spectacular style.'

In 2014, their marriage failed. She said she knew the failure ran deeper than the broken marriage, though. She didn't know what changes were needed in her life, but she knew that there had to be some. And that was when, she told me, she started to learn about failure.

*

If you're a sportsperson, you're going to fail a lot. In every match there are two teams, and even with a skill edge, a preparation edge and a psychological edge, you're going to lose a lot of the time. So you have to be prepared to lose, prepared to fail.

How do we prepare ourselves for failure? One of the things Elizabeth stressed in our interview is that we should all try not to become enmeshed with our failures; that we must create distance between ourselves and our failures. With that distance, we're more likely to see things for what they are and better recognise what our role is in our failures – and how that role can change us, if it needs to at all.

'A lot of people wrongly believe failure defines them when it happens, but actually failure more often than not is something that happens to you,' said Elizabeth. 'We think we *are* our failures, but usually failure is just something that happens to us. It's like anxiety – I am not my anxiety, it's just something that happens to me. When you recognise that, you place distance between yourself and your failure, and that gives you a little bit of distance and a little bit of breathing time.'

Elizabeth said failure can wrap itself around us, become part of us, and drag us down into a spiral of shame and doubt. Our failures cannot be ignored, but they have to be seen for what they are: things that have simply happened. She said we don't want failure to become an unresolved ghost, emerging to haunt us when we least want it to.

Good athletes know that failure isn't as important nor as defining as the bounce back. We ask ourselves, *What information have I gleaned? What's the path forward?* Instead of dwelling on the failure, letting it drag us down, these questions give us agency to make sure next time we are less likely to fail. Dealing with our failures better than our opponents gives us an advantage, just like having better bowlers or batters is to a team's advantage.

I think the most successful people frame their failures as opportunities instead of setbacks. Author and former SEAL member, Jocko Willink, writes about this, saying that whenever he suffers a failure he reframes it as 'good' and then looks for a path forward. That technique applies equally as well in cricket. So we lost a match? Good – here's an opportunity to evaluate where we went wrong.

Elizabeth said much the same thing. Distance is one of the keys to failing well, she told me, and in that distance, decisions can be made and lessons can be learned. 'After you fail comes a very important moment and also the true test of your character. That's how you respond.' She added, 'I didn't know it, but the [divorce] was an opportunity to build the life I wanted and not the one that I'd developed from social conditioning and 1980s romcoms and my own family.'

\*

After her divorce, Elizabeth Day decided to move to Los Angeles. Having been to LA a number of times for interviews, she thought it would be the perfect place to reset her life. It was a sunny and happy place, somewhere she could write outside, but most importantly it was a place where no one knew her except for one beloved and unjudging cousin.

Elizabeth pitched to her employer, *The Observer*, that she might move to LA on a semi-permanent basis to do movie junkets, celebrity interviews and lifestyle pieces. The paper agreed. 'LA comes in for so much bad press, but it can really provide this space where the hierarchies are a lot flatter. There's a hierarchy of money and power, but there isn't the insidiousness of the class system, which I now realise was quite stultifying.' Elizabeth noticed the English class structure far more when she was away from it, and in LA she recognised how pervasive it really was. LA was different – everybody was ready to be approached, everybody would accept a meeting, everybody was ready to tell an English stranger their life story.

Elizabeth said she'd been getting professional therapy before she went to Los Angeles, but it was only there that she started speaking freely about it. She loved the fact that people overshared in LA and regularly used 'therapy language' – and that this language was even being used in a new type of media centred around LA, where most of the best podcasts were recorded.

Podcasting started to boom around that time. 'Radio on demand on your phone' was how people were describing podcasting, which wasn't quite right. Podcasting was on demand, and it was available on phones, but it wasn't really radio. Podcasting was audio, but the format was different to radio shows. The popular podcasts were more informal, conversational and confessional than radio broadcasts.

In LA, Elizabeth became a dedicated listener to the podcasts *WTF with Marc Maron* (whom she interviewed for *The Observer*), *Where Should We Begin?* with psychotherapist Esther Perel, and *Serial*, a series about a potentially unsolved murder. *Serial* has a foundation of investigative journalism but also has the hosts talking about their feelings on the case and how their work was affecting them.

Eventually Elizabeth Day decided to produce her own limited podcast series about what could be learned from failure. That decision proven to be a very good one.

The idea for *How to Fail* came from her myriad failures, including her marriage, and from how much Elizabeth realised she had learned from those failures. She thought that her story of growth through failure might not be a unique one, and that investigating the failures of other thoughtful and articulate people might be fertile podcasting ground. In 2018, she recorded eight episodes in which she interviewed famous writers such as Dolly Alderton, Sebastian Faulks, David Nicholls and other people about failure in their lives and their work.

In the first episode, an interview with her friend Phoebe Waller-Bridge – the British actress and screenwriter who had just created the show *Fleabag* – Elizabeth mostly plays the role of a detached host, usually speaking only to tease out information and insights from her guest.

As the series goes on, she shares more of her own feelings and failures – something that, she told me, went against her personal and professional grain. Elizabeth said that journalistic writing, for her, had been about 'disintermediated dialogue' between the subject and the reader, and that as much as she inserted herself into her work, that 'self' was a journalistic creation, existing on the page and not in her skin. The podcast became a different beast.

Pretty much from the first episode, the feedback from listeners was that they wanted Elizabeth to share more of herself, which she did. When she did, there were more messages asking about her story. She told me this created a 'virtuous cycle', meaning the more she shared, the more praise she got for it, which meant she shared more. She said it was hard to do, though. 'I had to try to know myself, which I thought I did but I didn't. The best way to know yourself is by being vulnerable and embracing your vulnerability.'

This vulnerability fed back into Elizabeth's writing, which she said took on a more nakedly personal aspect. First came her novel *The Party*. Set in the heart of the world of Britain's modern societal elites, *The Party* is about class angst, repressed emotion, early middle age and deep sexual longing. Before her divorce, Elizabeth had already written three novels that had been moderately successful, but *The Party* was a runaway hit.

Then came even bigger success, with exceptional sales. Elizabeth wrote a book to accompany her podcast, also called *How to Fail* but with the tagline *Everything I've Ever Learned from Things Going Wrong.* Gone were the guests present in the podcast – instead, the book was deeply personal. While the book maintains a 'how to' construction, this is really a thin veil; at its heart it's a confessional autobiography, something Elizabeth said she could never have imagined writing in her twenties or married thirties.

While some of the chapters are breezy and jocular, there is real failure – and real pain – in others, and in those chapters you can feel Elizabeth attempting to write her way to serenity. In that writing and in her podcast, she said she was trying to find herself, an authentic self, the person she could be for the rest of her life. She added that her failures were important catalysts for her to do that.

\*

Elizabeth's words really resonated with me when she spoke about how her podcast and memoir became spaces where vulnerability and honesty could breathe. I found it comparable to my experience with the interviews I've done for this book and with the book as a whole. Even writing now, it feels good to be able to take the time to say what I want to say.

A lot of the public speaking I do is at press conferences and media engagements or in short interviews. Of course, I'm happy to fulfil my media obligations, and sometimes I'm actually excited to be able to offer my perspective on a match or series. But much like Julia Gillard, I wear an armour of sorts when I go into these speaking engagements and I have learned to be guarded. Usually I stop a little short of what I might like to say.

Over my career, I've learned to be somewhat wary. Or maybe 'wary' isn't the right word – maybe it's 'aware'. As my career has progressed and I've had more exposure to the media, I've become more aware of where my speech might end up. I've seen more than a few storms in teacups, and when I speak publicly, like Julia, I'm already imagining the form in which my words may be used in articles, radio grabs and TV spots. Ultimately, you can't control the context in which the things you've said are used, but you can control what you say, so I do. I'm not necessarily proud to say that, but a big series or World Cup is taxing enough without added media scrutiny or attention.

Sometimes my team-mates and I are asked non-cricket questions, some about issues that might affect us. Whether or not we answer these questions is a matter of personal preference. There are some topics I don't feel well enough versed in to have a strong opinion on, but there are some subjects that affect me, and I feel a responsibility to answer honestly.

I'm on the record for being passionate about supporting climate change and the Indigenous Voice to Parliament.

With the leadership role and social media platform I have, I want to be a positive part of the conversation, supporting creative solutions. For some, that might make me 'Captain Woke' but for me it's just about wanting a better future for my kids and future generations.

We have a diverse bunch of lads with differing opinions within our team. After all, the only things that necessarily connect us are cricketing ability and citizenship. We are connected, though. We know, respect and really like each other. We're different men, often with quite different opinions, and yet we all generally get along and manage to accommodate and accept all those opinions. I've never captained a bad bloke – it's just that we all come from different places, with different histories and perspectives. In our environment, we see these differing personalities and opinions as a strength. Of course there are some healthy disagreements, and some mistakes made, but we all move on.

I often wish that there was more of an allowance for respectful failure in public discourse. There's a lot to be said for being more respectfully direct, more colloquial, maybe even more vulnerable in press conferences and speeches. But it's risky if you get it wrong, unintentionally causing offence, judged as too flippant. It takes bravery and a bit of latitude to fail.

When you speak privately with your mates, there's space for getting it wrong, learning from it, and growing as a person. Not so in public, where a mistaken opinion said with the best of intentions can sometimes play back as a media bite for years to come.

If we all had a little more tolerance and understanding in the public space, as we might for things said in private, everyone would be in a better place overall.

It's not a perfect metaphor, but in much the same way, we try to keep an open mind in our team and de-stress 'failure' as much as we can. When you pick someone for the team, you tell them you're going to stick by them and give them a long run. Otherwise, the pressure that comes from worrying about failing can potentially become a self-fulfilling prophecy and cause them to fail. Without that pressure, they're giving themselves the best chance to fulfil their potential.

This is also a better way to live. If you're always worried about failing every moment of your life, and if failing is a cliff you can't come back from, you're going to live your whole life with an elevated heart rate and associated sense of anxiety.

\*

Playing sport gives you permission to constantly re-evaluate how you're going, which gives you clarity as to what you are doing that is or isn't working. In John Bertrand's chapter, I talked a little about our approach to the 2023 World Cup, and my conversation with Elizabeth reminded me about some of the themes that arose from that.

Just as John reframed what success was for the Australian swimming team – personal bests over podium placings – when our team approached the World Cup we reframed what success and failure would look like to us. We knew it would be impossible to win every game. That kind of win ratio is not only unrealistic, but entirely out of our control. What we could control, however, was how we played the game, in terms of style, tactics, identity and approach. We'd already identified that an aggressive or creative approach would give us a chance to set ourselves apart from the rest of the pack. We thought this approach might also improve our odds against some of the stronger oppositions, where our win ratio is normally around 50:50. By playing this way, the wins tend to be more fabulous but so are the losses, which can bring added scrutiny.

We didn't want that scrutiny to hold us back though, when we knew in our guts that it was the right call, so we decided that 'failing' would no longer be about losing games. We would only be disappointed in our performance if we didn't stick to our tactics, if we let the pressure and stress and exhaustion push us back into playing it safe. In cricket, if you play it safe and edge the ball and get out, it's considered an acceptable out. You played it safe, played the right shot, but it was just a good ball. Whereas if you hit a big shot and get caught somewhere out in the field, it's considered a bad shot, an unacceptable risk. The reality is that the person who blocked the ball wasn't going to make any difference, even if they middled it, but at least the other shot was trying to score some runs and move the game forward. Tradition says the first is a more acceptable out, even if on balance you're going to lose a lot more games doing that.

We decided to flip that mindset. If we were going to lose, we were at least going to lose spectacularly, and on our own terms.

Now that isn't to say that destigmatising failure makes losing hurt any less. Elizabeth knows this, perhaps better than many.

I was so impressed by Elizabeth's bravery and candour in our conversation. I had never met her before this journey, and yet I found myself reciprocating almost immediately. Her openness allowed me to open up in return.

It can be a bit taboo to speak about our failures, but Elizabeth's podcast is all about speaking about those things that are hardest. I was especially moved when Elizabeth candidly talked about what she considers to be her signature failure: her failure, time and time again, to have a baby. It's a failure that, according to her, has affected her the most – for worse, but also for better. 'I feel like I found my calling in life, which is to speak about infertility and associated issues,' she said.

Elizabeth has written about infertility in non-fiction and fiction, spoken about it on podcasts, and even had one of her infertility experiences end up in *Fleabag*. (It's a scene where the main character's sister disappears at dinner, and when she's found, she bellows, 'No, just get your hands off my miscarriage. It's mine.')

Elizabeth's failure to have a baby started, like so many of our failures do, with a deeply embedded assumption. 'I had always somewhat lazily and ignorantly assumed I would have children,' she said. 'My whole sex education in school was entirely devoted to not getting pregnant.' She added that when she was younger, she assumed pregnancy was always just one choice away and she never thought about infertility. She was on a contraceptive pill for fourteen years and said, 'When I went off the pill I thought I'd have triplets.'

Elizabeth stopped taking the pill shortly after getting married. As per the plan she'd set for herself in life, now was the time to get knocked up. Yet cycle after cycle, she was disappointed. After two years of trying, she put herself in the hands of a fertility doctor, who ran a series of tests before giving her what she calls 'the most useless diagnosis imaginable': a case of 'unexplained infertility'. There was no apparent reason why she couldn't conceive, but it was recommended that she start in vitro fertilisation (IVF), a process that begins with stimulating the ovulatory process to produce viable ova, or eggs.

Elizabeth went through two back-to-back IVF cycles, but in each instance she barely produced any eggs. She wanted to know why, and a lot more besides. She didn't want to just be a slave to information given to her by doctors or by medical texts that were often unintelligible to her. 'I remember going to find a book about IVF … and I couldn't find one. There are shelves and shelves of parenting and baby books, but none about IVF.' She wanted to learn and to share but found nowhere to do it. 'I became very lost and lonely, especially in my marriage, which in retrospect should have been a red flag.'

While taking a break from IVF, Elizabeth became pregnant out of the blue. In an early scan, she heard the heartbeat of a foetus. Afterwards, she found, 'The world treats you differently. The world seems bounteous … and it feels like you're in the class of the blessed.' Everything was momentarily okay. Life was momentarily okay. Her marriage was momentarily okay. Then it was all over.

Elizabeth started bleeding, and a few days before her three-month scan discovered the heartbeat had disappeared. 'This was a very traumatic experience and the lowest I've ever felt,' she said. 'I had a year of hormonal insanity and crushed hope and losses and grief and mild depression, and then my marriage ended.'

At age thirty-eight, Elizabeth started a relationship with a man in his twenties. With their age difference in mind, she decided to freeze her eggs. Doctors told her that, given her age, they expected to be able to extract fifteen viable eggs to be fertilised later. Doctors only managed to extract two viable eggs, and one other that was potentially viable – and besides, just before her thirty-ninth birthday, Elizabeth's relationship ended.

'Then I really felt fucked,' she told me. 'Going back to what I said earlier about curiosity about life, I wanted to understand everything.' She said that the understanding she really wanted was how parenting could bring meaning to life. She thought not being able to quench that curiosity might be unbearable.

Elizabeth was alone, and so far from her goal that she despaired again. She was forced to think about the possibility that she'd never achieve the goal that seemed ultimate – and when thinking about that, she had to consider why it had been a goal all along. Yes, it was part of the confected vision of the future built by social norms and eighties romcoms in her childhood, but there was more to it. She said, 'I felt fervently that when I had a child, it would give my life meaning, that things would make sense and things would clarify and silly things would become less worrisome. I had a desire to build a family of love and connection, because those are the things I think I'm good at.'

Nearing forty, Elizabeth looked at a life beyond the goal of having a child; a life where her capacity for love and connection might have to be expressed elsewhere. She started online dating, and on the Hinge app she met her now husband, the tech CEO Justin Basini. He has children from a previous marriage, and Elizabeth said she was beginning to wonder if the only experience she would have of children would be as a stepmother, aunt, friend and godmother. 'I thought I was coming to terms with the fact I would never have one of my own – and then I got pregnant just before my forty-first birthday. We saw the pregnancy as a gift and miracle. That pregnancy ended as a miscarriage, but it had made us realise how much we wanted it.'

Elizabeth told me that if her partner had in any way been wary about the idea of having a child, she would have stopped, and the dream would have been over, but Basini was just as enamoured as she was. The pair hired another fertility expert, who recommended a surgery on what they said was Elizabeth's irregularly shaped womb. After the surgery, COVID started to take hold, and the day after the lockdown began in London, Elizabeth found out she was pregnant. At an early scan there was again a strong, healthy heartbeat, but a week later – at a scan organised due to the sonographer finding the foetus slightly on the small side –

the heartbeat was gone. 'That pregnancy was medically managed,' she told me.

This was the third of Elizabeth's three experiences of miscarriage. The first had been a dilatation and curettage operation, the second was left to happen naturally and this third one was medically managed at home, meaning she opted to take pills, which gave her some of the worst pain she'd ever had. The only other option during the pandemic was to leave the miscarriage to happen naturally but that meant carrying around her baby for an unspecified amount of time, which Elizabeth shared, was a psychological load she couldn't even begin to fathom. 'It was pain like I've never felt before.'

Afterwards, the pair kept trying. 'It felt like it was a test about how much we wanted it,' said Elizabeth. 'I thought I had an obligation to try everything to live without regret.'

The pair married, and with Elizabeth now forty-three they decided to try to get pregnant using an egg donor. Eventually they ended up with two viable embryos. The couple had a seemingly perfect transplant. Elizabeth said she then spent the first two weeks of 2023 convinced she was pregnant. 'I felt so pregnant. I've been pregnant, so I know what it feels like. It felt like that. The universe seemed to be sending me signs.'

It seemed that it had happened: Elizabeth was in love, married and – nearing an age when this would be very difficult for most women – possibly pregnant. Then she opened an email from her fertility clinic in the wake of a blood test. The email said that Elizabeth's blood did not show elevated levels of HCG (human chorionic gonadotropin), therefore she was not pregnant. 'It was totally shattering – all of that hope, just gone. I felt lied to on a cosmic scale ... and that's twelve years of the journey.' Elizabeth said this with a laugh, having told some of her story in tears.

It took Elizabeth about a year to accept that her failure was complete and that she will never be a mother. But, she added, in that year her disappointment became hope. 'I feel such peace now, in a way. I thought [after accepting I won't have a child] my life would have to change in such a dramatic way, but I haven't had to. My life has just been enhanced. Embracing the idea of a future without a baby has opened up all this space for creativity.'

Elizabeth now feels compelled to speak and write about infertility in a way that would have helped her in the past decade and half. She said she wants to fill a gap in the information market for the millions of people who can't have children or haven't had children but want to. 'I guess I was struggling with the idea of legacy, that which you leave the world with, something that's a part of you that's forever there,' she told me. 'Well, books are legacy, too, and podcasts. I connect with people through those things, and they make me feel connected. Through them I feel that I have love to give.'

Elizabeth's latest novel, *Magpie* – her most popular – is about infertility, but it's not at all what you might expect. 'I always want to write about fertility in a way it hasn't been written about before. *How to Fail* was pure non-fiction ...

this is what it is, but there are so many other things you can do in fiction that can be very cathartic.'

*Magpie* is about a couple trying to have a baby, but it is also about a lodger who comes into their home to help pay the mortgage – and who may be a covetous psychopath. 'I wanted it to be a thriller, as there's so much about [infertility] treatment that makes you feel unhinged and that you're losing it, but you have to keep that hope alive. So many of those feelings and emotions lend [themselves] to a thriller – that there's something chaotic and unhinged, and like you're being drawn into something.'

Elizabeth published the non-fiction book *Friendaholic: Confessions of a Friendship Addict*, in which she talks about the lack she felt in her life, and the longing to have a child. She told me that lack and longing were defining characteristics of most of her life, but, 'I don't feel any of those things anymore. [I thought having a child was my purpose,] but my purpose is to speak for those people who have tried and failed. My purpose is to reassure people that there's so much growth and love and wisdom from not getting what you thought you wanted.'

*

I was so inspired by Elizabeth's story and her point that failure is universal. Everyone fails all the time, but because we so often shout our successes and whisper our failures, we can very often imagine that we and only we are the ones who are failing, while everyone else is living a life of endless success. She added that part of the reason she wants to talk about her infertility is to reveal her own failure, which from the outside couldn't have been seen.

'My thirties was such a period of intense transition, but if you only knew me professionally or if you only knew me from afar, you wouldn't have understood any of that,' she said. 'I was feeling such a failure every day, but I kept it secret from so many people. You just never know what internal battles someone is fighting. We compare our perfectly curated outsides with our messy neurotic insides, and it's a disconnect I'm keen on breaking down.'

Elizabeth told me she's interested not only in helping people to be more accepting of failure and more capable of bouncing back from it, but also in pointing out the inevitability of failure – not as a depressing thought but as a hopeful one. 'Even if we were to become completely understanding and wise and connected with the divine energies around us, even then failure would still happen. That's something I find really beautiful. In every failure you're acquiring knowledge and data. Even if that data is just: "This hurts" or "I can survive it." At the end, failure can be a thing that connects us and invites us to be vulnerable, and I'm all about vulnerability.'

The time I spent chatting with Elizabeth Day some of the most challenging, confronting and honest of those interviews I have done for this book. I loved it, though, not only because she was so honest and articulate, but also because of how relatable and important her advice on failing was – learning from it when you can, moving on from it when you can't, but accepting it always, and never letting it define you. Some truths are universal. They defy class, gender, upbringing and life experience.

I guess I could look like someone who hasn't experienced much failure in my life, but of course I have. I spent a lot of time in the wilderness after first being picked to play for Australia. Much of this was due to injury, but a part of me considered those injuries to be personal failings, given that I had defined myself by my ability to play cricket.

Cricketers – and a lot of sportspeople – are often better at failing than most, because it's an inherent part of sport. Good cricketers do everything they can to avoid failure, training and preparing as best they can, but good cricketers also know that's not always going to be enough. Incidentally, the best coaches know this too; some of the worst coaches I've had were the ones who yelled and raged any time their team lost.

So much of cricket, like so much of life, is defined by luck. Take a batter who edges to the keeper in single digits, and another who gives the same edge – only to have the keeper drop the ball – and then goes on for a hundred. Should one batter be derided and the other exalted?

When we succeed, we assume our own role has been exemplary, ignoring any role luck may have played and often continuing as we had before. When we fail, we often self-search. In the wake of failure we are more likely to search for shortcomings, accept radical change and question entire paradigms. When we fail, we're usually presented with new opportunities, and invited to understand how luck plays a role in everything we do.

When you begin to see failure as an opportunity for learning, new possibilities open up. For example, if you always treat a nets session as if it were a real game, as some selectors and coaches do, then you lose the chance to use it in many other valuable ways. In that respect, it can become an unhealthy form of training, where failure can stress you out and cause you to lock up in a real game. Whereas if you treat nets as a place where failure is accepted or even expected, it becomes a healthy place to experiment and test new techniques in a controlled environment. Just as we use conditioning to test our limits, nets can be used to tinker with or try out new shots, and fail in order to discover.

I'm not saying every nets session should be like this – there's also value in using it as a high-intensity match simulation in the lead-up to a game – but it's important to define what success and failure look like before you set out on any endeavour, and have the courage to stick to those definitions.

Failure of any sort is almost always unpleasant at the time, but there is a hell of a lot to learn from it. Success is a destination, while failure is a journey – one on which growth, learning and improvement can happen.

# 9

## Serendipity isn't just knowing when to take an opportunity, but also knowing when to walk away

*A conversation with Ronnie Screwvala*

INDIA IS AN AMAZING PLACE, ONE THAT IS INARGUABLY the centre of gravity for cricket. A survey conducted by the ICC in 2018 found that, of the one billion cricket fans in the world, ninety per cent are Indian. Young and old, men and women, Indians embrace the game like the people of no other country, and with India's economy continuing to boom, it's safe to say that it will continue to be the centre of the game for a long time, and a place Australian cricketers will continue to travel to with regularity.

As a boy, I never would have imagined I'd end up travelling to India dozens of times. Getting to know this fascinating country has been one of the unexpected joys of my career. I love the food, the culture, the people and their passion – especially for cricket – but the thing I have loved the most is how dynamic their country is.

Every time I visit India I am invigorated. There are new cricket grounds, new office towers, new roads, new airports and new sponsors. In the time since I was born, Indian GDP per capita has increased more than tenfold (by comparison, Australia's has grown just over three times in my lifetime) and total Indian GDP has doubled roughly every five years for decades. That kind of rapid growth changes a country in more ways than can be seen from the window of a team bus. When a country has that kind of growth, it creates a lot of risk, but it also provides enormous opportunities for people who find a way to seize them. Those opportunities usually foster a dynamic class of entrepreneurs at the crest of the surging economic wave, creating enormous fortunes for some and leaving others far behind.

It's also something that changes the cultural landscape of a country, and if there's anything Indians love more than cricket, it might just be cinema. More films are made in India than anywhere else in the world, and around the world, Indian films are watched by more people than any other type of film. It's estimated that for decades about ninety per cent of the Indian population regularly visit the cinema, both in India and overseas; in fact, many Indian films make more money in Australia than Australian films do. Bollywood isn't just a multibillion-dollar business in India, it's part of the cultural firmament.

One person leading the charge in that changing landscape is Rohinton 'Ronnie' Screwvala, the founder of one of India's most powerful media companies, a former managing director of Disney India and a producer of literally hundreds of Bollywood films. He has all the accolades you'd expect of a titan of industry: he's been named one of *Time* magazine's 100 Most Influential People in the World and one of *Fortune*'s Most Powerful 25 People in Asia, but he didn't start at the top. It was only through serendipity, passion and the awareness of which opportunities to grasp and which to leave behind that he has made it so far.

I met with Ronnie in the ITC Grand Central, Mumbai, the morning of a game. He came to the hotel and we snuck into a quiet conference room next to the restaurant – perhaps the only quiet place in Mumbai – to have a coffee.

I found Ronnie to be a pragmatic person, and eternally curious to talk to others and learn from them. Our conversation wasn't one-sided, and I felt like he had come to learn just as much from me as I'd hoped to learn from him. It was Ronnie who asked me the first question, wanting to know how I'd found out about him. I told him it was through a mutual friend of my manager and then asked him why someone of his level of accomplishment agreed to speak with me. He replied that he thought it was an interesting project, and he doesn't get a chance to speak to an Australian cricket captain every day, 'so I thought I should say yes.'

I like that he gives credit to others where it is due for his success – primarily to his wife and other creative partners – and that he has never lost sight of that. There is a real curiosity and humility in him too. He credits serendipity for a part of his success, but also recognises that he's worked really hard to get to where he is.

\*

Ronnie was born in 1956, less than a decade after Indian independence and partition, and he grew up in a middle-class family in Mumbai. He started his academic life in an underprivileged school, changing to a more elite one after his father found employment at a British pharmaceutical company.

Ronnie studied hard and gained acceptance into the Sydenham College of Commerce and Economics, which he said he initially found easy, attempting to cram his four-year course into three. But, after failing one of those years, he had to repeat it. 'I had been very arrogant, and failing taught me a lot,' he said. 'That was when I realised that if I got into a profession, I just wasn't going to be successful building someone else's vision. I needed to work on my own.'

Ronnie boldly told his parents that, after university, he wanted to become an entrepreneur. Keep in mind that this conversation happened in the seventies, when India had no investment framework, private equity or start-up culture. 'It was scary for my parents when I told them,' said Ronnie. His father asked him to at least 'do an MBA and have something to fall back on,' but Ronnie didn't want to have a fall-back position, because he thought that if he did, he may be too tempted to take it when things got difficult. His father cautioned him: 'If things go south, just know I won't be able to bail you out because I don't have the resources to bail you out.'

At the time, Ronnie was earning some money as a semi-professional stage actor and part-time television host, but it wasn't much. 'That limited the type of business that I could try to build,' he said. That was when serendipity first touched Ronnie's life.

Ronnie is a clever businessman and a great communicator who doesn't ordinarily repeat himself, but 'serendipity' is a word he uses often. It is, he told me, a concept that has been central to his success. He described serendipity as the gift or aptitude for finding and making desirable discoveries by accident. It is not just about luck and the world presenting opportunities to you: it's about having your eyes wide open so that, should there be an opportunity, you'll be the one to benefit from it.

This is true of Ronnie's story, and it's also true of most people's luck. Nobody can generate luck, but I think the people who seem luckiest are those who are open to opportunities, and then grab those opportunities with both hands and squeeze as much juice out of them as possible. That, to my mind, is serendipity.

My conversation with Ronnie made me wonder if there are things you can do to be more serendipitous. Can you be someone who finds or makes their own luck in business, sport or life? And is serendipity about having a creative vision, like Ronnie, or is it about being open to opportunities as they come? I suspect it's a bit of both.

Before you can start thinking about how to take advantage of each opportunity that comes your way, you have to know where you want to go and what path you might take to get there. Then you put yourself in the best position you can for that vision to be realised. A bear doesn't know exactly where a salmon is going to jump, but it's more likely to catch fish in the river than on the bank. A fielder doesn't know where their catches may come, but standing where a batter usually likes to hit is a good start.

In Ronnie's case, serendipity placed an opportunity before him that allowed him to overlap his ambition to build something successful and lasting with his passion for theatre and media.

Indians might be mad for media, but when Ronnie graduated from uni there was just one TV station in India to watch: the government-owned and operated Doordarshan. 'Televisions weren't even sold with a remote in India,' Ronnie said, 'because there wasn't a second channel to change to.' At the same time, VHS tapes had recently become available, and Indian law had not yet forbidden the recording and rebroadcasting of television programs, even for commercial purposes. Ronnie saw an opportunity to record already aired Doordarshan programming and then rebroadcast those shows on local networks within apartment blocks in Mumbai, with his subscribers paying for the privilege.

It was not an immediate success. Far from it – for the first year, Ronnie's business was an abject failure. 'It was a lot of rejection and, in fact, a lot of physical rejection, as the business required going from door to door, and doors were often being slammed,' said Ronnie. He also found, when he tried to hire high-quality, ambitious, young staff, that *he* was often the one being interviewed: most of the interviewees asked Ronnie to sit down with their parents so he could explain to them what this media sector was and how it might eventually benefit their child.

Ronnie and his team went from apartment to apartment, and the business began to slowly build over a few years. But he saw that his ambitions would surpass the possible growth of his business. 'Going forward, I knew the law was going to be grey. If I needed to expand, I'd need to start laying cable [between buildings]' – something that, according to the law, only the government could do. 'I realised I needed to move on, to capture some value, generate some seed capital and start something new.'

This is something else I find incredible about Ronnie's success. More than his ability to build up successful companies is his aptitude for knowing when to walk away.

It's so hard to create and build something. And when you have, it's often even harder to hand it over to someone else. At this point, after some success, do you double down and roll the dice again? It's a bit like a cricketer stuck in the middle of their career, puttering along having some success but perhaps plateauing. Do you innovate your game dramatically to try and take it to the next level, or are you too afraid of the possibility of going backwards in doing so? Do you set up a Test match to try and win it but risk a loss, or do you drag it out to ensure a draw is the most likely outcome?

This is where a cognitive bias called 'loss aversion' comes into play. This psychological phenomenon essentially boils down to a simple idea: the pain of losing something is twice as powerful as the pleasure of winning that same thing. Because of this, people will go out of their way to avoid loss, but they won't go to the same lengths to achieve the same gain. This misvaluing of loss and gain tempts people to play things safe – whether that's a shot in cricket or an opportunity in life – when the reality is they might be better off over the long run taking the riskier path.

We'd learned this lesson the hard way in a round game in the 2021 T20 World Cup. We'd got off to a slow start against England, and in order to try and not lose too badly we limped to a score of 125, which was then chased down in 11 overs. It was a thumping. By being so loss averse, we had achieved exactly what we had been hoping to avoid! From then on, we vowed to not fall in the trap of playing timidly again.

Amazon's CEO, Jeff Bezos, talks about a regret minimisation framework he uses to assist in his decision-making. He visualises himself twenty years in the future, looking back on the moment of decision, and then asks himself, 'What decision that I take now will I regret less in twenty years?' I like to use this thinking framework when looking for a path forward. The answer I almost always come back to is that I'll never look back in hindsight and wish I'd been more timid.

Ronnie doesn't play it safe. He wanted to focus on being an entrepreneur, and knew that having a fall-back might tempt him to use it. Instead, he stuck to his vision and never allowed himself to become distracted from his path by a safer option.

This is the true magic of Ronnie's success. As he was considering a sale of his business, his right-hand man told him he was planning to leave to try to develop a similar endeavour. Ronnie asked him, 'Would you like to take the business with you?' They arrived at a price, and Ronnie moved on. Using the cash equivalent of about AU$1000, he started a new business, UTV Software Communications, which would end up being one of the most valuable media businesses in India, with an enterprise value of more than AU$2 billion, and which would eventually channel Ronnie's passion for theatre into success.

*

As a young man, Ronnie had found a passion for theatre. He worked as an actor at the Bombay Theatre, performing English-language classics, and one of his first real jobs was hosting a show on Doordarshan. He loved the storytelling of theatre, the language and the ability for a text to capture both the imagination and the audience. He said he loved theatre people too – not only his fellow actors, but the directors, producers and designers who together created a package that could be promoted and sold.

Ronnie had thought his time on the stage would simply be a diversion from his future career as a businessman, but that wasn't the case. 'The maturity and reflexes that theatre teaches you are very good,' he said. 'You are alone in front of an audience for two hours, and it gives you a lot of confidence.' Just as important in his career was the passion he built for the theatre, and the understanding of what words on the page of a script were going to become a hit.

UTV started small, creating in-flight and educational videos for a handful of clients, before producing some scripted content. The company became well regarded, especially for a popular daily soap opera it produced for Doordarshan. Then in 1991, satellite television came to India, creating massive opportunities for UTV, and it grew steadily in scale, becoming known for its quality and attention to detail. It was, according to Ronnie, a company built for the future. Potential partners often sniffed around, looking to acquire the company, but Ronnie wasn't looking to be bought: 'I wanted to list the company and build it as a brand. If you want to build a brand … you have to do it with a [business-to-consumer] model.' He wanted UTV to become a distributor with its own television channels, but he also wanted its content to be on big screens across the country. 'The only thing that gets Indians really fired up outside of cricket is movies,' he said.

Ronnie gets really fired up by movies. He spun off UTV Motion Pictures from its parent company in the nineties, and their first film hit Indian cinemas in 1994. The film wasn't disastrously bad, but it was a financial failure, having little or no cut-through. 'Our first five movies were a disaster,' he said. 'We thought we understood creativity and we understood the consumers, but we didn't. In retrospect we were trying to do what everyone else did. The problem was they were doing it ten times better than we were.'

The UTV board eventually told Ronnie, 'You have to get out of this business,' but he refused. His passions were embedded in UTV Motion Pictures, as a businessman and a creative, and he was heavily involved in each major project. 'I consider myself a creative catalyst,' he told me, adding that he loves being in this role and wanted to work with India's best directors, writers, actors and musicians. He had a significant passion for cinema, and besides, he believed that if he wanted to build a serious Indian media brand, he couldn't just back out of the biggest part of the business, tail between his legs. He knew that there's no real formula for what works in a movie. The only sustainable thing is to keep evolving and changing, even if you get some flops amid the successes. In cricket you have to take big risks to have a big hit, and Ronnie was similarily going to keep going, boom or bust.

'Our penny-drop moment,' he told me, 'was knowing we were the outsiders in the movie industry and that we should be looking at newer segments [in the market].'

Indian cinema was at the time defined by distinctive genres, be they hazy romances, moral family dramas or apolitical action extravaganzas, and UTV had tried to follow the conventions but quickly realised they weren't going to survive just by following trends that other people had established. The history of the Indian film industry showed that it had long offered success to those who could get ahead of the nation's moods. After independence, the most successful films had been bright, happy musicals. When Ronnie had been at university, during the national state of emergency in the country and at a time of rising international tensions, paranoid outsider action flicks had dominated. Ronnie wondered what was happening in India then. How did young moviegoers want to see themselves on the screen? Along with one of UTV's partners, a production manager named Zarina Mehta (who would become Zarina Screwvala when she and Ronnie married), Ronnie began a focus-group research project that would inform what kinds of movies would be greenlit.

Rather than delegate this research to consultants or sending a junior staff member out, Ronnie and Zarina mostly did the work themselves. How else to get a gauge of what was and wasn't working?

They asked young people – especially at universities – not about what kind of movies they wanted to see, but rather how they felt about their lives and the economy, and how their own political participation might affect the country.

The result of this research – and the point from which UTV Motion Pictures turned its fortunes around – was *Rang De Basanti*, a movie in which a British filmmaker comes to India in the 1930s to make a film about Indian freedom fighters but becomes enmeshed with a group of Indian students who are fighting to uncover corruption. It has action and romance, and a thumping soundtrack from A.R. Rahman, who'd have huge success across the world a couple of years later writing music for *Slumdog Millionaire*.

*Rang De Basanti* is a great film in any language, and I'm not the only one who thinks so. The film was a massive commercial success, and a critical one too, collecting a number of major Indian film awards. From there, UTV

Motion Pictures only grew, with Ronnie producing fourteen films in two years, including an American film starring Chris Rock.

UTV's brand value had also started to grow on the small screen after it launched a series of specialised satellite channels, the most popular of which was Hungama TV, a kids' channel that out-rated the large international brands that had launched in India.

Serendipity knocked again as the Disney Corporation, with an eye on the exploding Indian media market, approached UTV and asked to buy Hungama TV. Ronnie told them he wasn't looking to sell part of his business, and Disney came back with another offer: they would buy a minority stake in all of UTV, allowing Ronnie to continue to run the business as he saw fit. It was an offer Ronnie couldn't ignore: a lot of money from an investor who was asking for little control. That deal was inked the same year as *Rang De Basanti* hit cinemas and, for the seven years that followed, the relationship between UTV and Disney thrived.

Ronnie told me he would have been happy to continue for another seven years and seven more after that, but according to him, '[Disney] wanted to put it all together and run it, so one day they popped the question': may we buy everything? It would be, by far, Disney's largest ever acquisition outside the US. They wanted the company, and they also wanted Ronnie, building into the deal an agreement that would see him installed as the managing director of the Walt Disney Company India.

He hadn't been looking to sell, before Disney made their offer. He'd have been happy to run UTV for the rest of his life. But the offer that Disney made was two or three times the price he believed he could have got if he were trying to sell the company. The opportunity was too enticing.

For the first time in his life, Ronnie was going to work for someone else.

*

Ever since Ronnie was young, he'd had a vision of where he wanted to go. He knew he had an entrepreneurial heart, seeing as an end goal a company that he had worked to fully mature and that allowed him to do the things he loved. In the wake of Disney's offer, he discovered he had finally realised that vision. As part of the deal, he had been offered golden handcuffs. If he worked for Disney for five years, building the business further, his remuneration would be staggering. 'I had full free rope to do what I wanted to do,' he said. 'And there was a serious upside if I could make this a billion-dollar revenue business in India for them.' All he had to do was work for someone else.

He just couldn't do it.

Ronnie was impressed by the way Disney worked, with the company having strong brand clarity, but this was also something he butted up against. One such instance was during the production of the film *Barfi!*, a family-friendly romantic comedy Ronnie believed was 'perfect for the Disney brand'. There's an integral scene in which a character smokes a cigarette, which was beyond Disney's brand guidelines. They wanted the scene cut, while the film's director was adamant that the scene must stay in. Ronnie advocated for the director, as he usually had throughout his career.

Another thing I like about Ronnie is that he always tries to keep creativity at the forefront of his business, and trusts his staff rather than get managerial and micromanage. Ronnie stuck to his decision, and *Barfi!* was released with the smoking scene ... but not by Disney. Instead, it was distributed by UTV Motion Pictures. The film was a runaway success, earning AU$30 million at the box office against its AU$6 million budget. It was also lauded at film awards and was India's official entry for the Best Foreign Language Film Oscar, vindicating Ronnie's decision to preference creativity over tradition.

Creativity sees its place in cricket too, but whenever you start to talk about being too creative, people can put their guard up. Most change-rooms are full of people who have played cricket since they could walk, and we all hold some dogma on the way certain things 'ought' to be done. People can get really caught up in any change in cricket. There's a reason the saying is, 'That's just not cricket.'

That's not to say that we should be creative just for creativity's sake – it should always be purposeful. It's like the old saying, 'Don't fix it if it isn't broken.' For instance, we're really lucky to have a consistent team right now, and have had for the last five years. For some of us, that length of time could be half our careers – half a generation of a cricket team coming up together.

One way we have pushed our boundaries is with how we consider data.

Data can get a bad rap in cricket, and sport in general, as it's seen as too rigid, not pure and subjective like we want our sport to be. However, data gives us a chance to be creative, to think differently to the crowd as long as we're approaching it the right way and asking the right questions. Ben Lexcen, the designer of *Australia II*, which John Bertrand sailed to victory in the America's Cup, relied heavily on data to inform his innovative winged keel design. Ronnie and Zarina relied on the data they collected to inform their production of *Rang De Basanti*.

We employ a data analyst, Tom Body, and always encourage him to throw us any findings he thinks the data suggests, but that we haven't thought of. By only concentrating on the objective, he can offer a fresh perspective on the game. Many of the times we'll talk through those ideas and discard them, but as I've found with so many things in this book, the key is to be open-minded. For example, in one instance Tom told us the data showed a strong correlation between me as a batter – who normally bats low – facing left-arm fast-bowling and perhaps I could be thrown to the top of the order. It made sense (by the data anyways), but we all agreed the sample size wasn't big enough to consider it further. Sometimes it's about balancing what could happen with the recognition that the data might not pan out.

Occasionally there are some crazy left-field ideas that we do use and they pay off. For instance, as an Australian team it's almost tradition that we play three quick bowlers, and we have three tall quick bowlers on our team. But sometimes the data suggests two spinners would be a better match-up against a particular team or on a particular pitch. So the data acts as a conversation starter, and either way, it's fertile ground for ideas in a world of cricketers who have done the same thing the same way for years on end.

In Ronnie's case, the only power he really had was to walk away, which is what he did. 'I was very frank at the end of the first year,' he said. 'I told [Disney Corporation CEO] Bob Iger: "I think Disney is a lovely brand and I'd pay $100 to go to Disneyland, but I can't see myself building Disney as a brand in India. I'm not the guy."'

Ronnie left Disney the next year, at age fifty-seven, and had to again think about what excited him and what he wanted to do next. 'I was leaving a lot on the table,' he told me. 'But to me, you don't get younger and you have to be excited about what you want to do with your life.'

Years before leaving Disney, while still building UTV, he had established a not-for-profit endeavour named Swades with Zarina, who had left UTV some years before. For more than a decade, Swades (which translates to 'our home' or 'homeland') was relatively small, with three full-time staff executing incisive projects that looked at improving education and health for rural Indians. Then, one day, Ronnie had a conversation with Zarina that drastically enlarged Swades' ambitions.

Zarina, whom Ronnie says is not only his life partner but the person he shares every creative decision with, had just undertaken a ten-day course hosted by a not-for-profit in which professionals and graduates prepared to do volunteer work at low-income schools. After the course, she announced that she was going to take a full-time placement at one of the schools. Ronnie argued that her – and their – ambitions might be expanded. With the skills they'd developed building UTV, and the money that it had generated, he suggested they could scale up their own not-for-profit instead. 'That was a dining-table conversation, and it was a really expensive one,' said Ronnie. 'I made the most expensive retention choices in my life and said, "Why don't we lift a million people out of poverty every six or seven years?"'

That suggestion became the guiding star of the improved Swades Foundation, which now concentrates on rural development in a holistic way, cooperatively improving education, health care, sanitation and economic development for the people of the Raigad and Nashik districts of Maharashtra state, where Mumbai is the capital. The foundation now has five thousand staff. According to an independent audit, it has improved conditions in over three thousand hamlets where more than a million people live, by building toilets and sanitation infrastructure, creating business opportunities though training, loans and irrigation, conducting medical screenings and surgeries, and – arguably the most important piece of the development pie – improving education for hundreds of thousands of students through investment, infrastructure and training.

The Swades idea of development is that all of these elements are essential for success, but education is the one element that is both empowering and regenerative, meaning that once you've educated people in the areas that Swades concentrates on, they are likely to help with other developmental problems.

This experience led Ronnie to cofound another venture, upGrad, in 2015. At the time, there wasn't an alternative to traditional university study in India. The idea of upGrad was that it could augment and replace other types of education, offering people already in the workplace the opportunity to do further study when it suited them best, and keeping Indian white-collar workers employable and trained in the latest skills and technologies. upGrad is distinct from other companies that are video-based and term-bound, relying instead on a mentoring system that could be started at any time.

In 2016, the company graduated its first students in a course on entrepreneurship and the development of start-up companies. By 2018, upGrad had ten thousand students. By 2020, it had a million. It is now the most valuable education company in India, with a valuation of roughly AU$3 billion (greater than UTV ever had). It offers certification courses all the way up to PhDs, concentrating on the 'careers of tomorrow', such as data science, digital marketing, AI and machine learning. But beyond the valuation and growth of the company, Ronnie said he's still fully engaged with upGrad because it contributes to India.

Ronnie Screwvala is a great example of a businessperson who doesn't chase profits and growth at the expense of the bigger picture. He recognises the value of growth, innovation and business, but he also recognises that the *direction* of that growth and innovation is important too. He told me, 'In my own small way I feel that online education is making India a developed country, because I think we need to do that. And I think the not-for-profit is raising aspirations in India.'

He sees his work as a film producer through this lens too. Now the head of RSVP Movies (established after his non-compete clause with Disney ended), Ronnie is again making successful films and series, in between his obligations as the head of his other companies. 'Some people like to play golf in their spare time – I like to make movies,' he said with a laugh.

Ronnie speaks with such gusto about the films and other media he's produced. Films aren't just line items to him, created in service of a healthier balance sheet. They're obviously intended to make a profit, but they aren't made solely for that purpose. They're his love, and in the service of making better films and more accessible media, Ronnie became a billionaire along the way. He said his hope is that Indian cinema might contribute to Indian soft power, in the way that British and American cultural exports have become powerful diplomatic assets. 'Look at American action films,' he said. 'That country hasn't won a war for seventy years, but you wouldn't know it watching their films.'

*

Ronnie's story – turning his love of theatre into a business that was first small, then medium, then large, and eventually titanic – is an incredible one.

Anyone who can build a company as large as UTV from nothing is impressive, but it is particularly exceptional that he built his billion-dollar media empire from a start in theatre in Mumbai, with no real financial backing, through sheer grit, resolve, determination and a lot of self-made luck.

After selling to Disney and walking away from UTV, it must have been difficult for Ronnie to imagine what might come next. Playing professional cricket is a similarly all-encompassing job. I've often found it hard to imagine what my life will look like when my career ends. I can imagine a lot of other professional athletes and people in high-powered roles like Ronnie's (like Julia Gillard after she retired from politics) might fear what comes next too, when the frenetic, important, adrenaline-inducing day-to-day demands of their positions disappear. Not Ronnie. Well practised at that side of serendipity, when it came time to sell UTV, and then to walk away from Disney, he just did it.

How he managed this – how he broke away from the goal he'd been fixated on from an early age – is twofold. First, Ronnie has an entrepreneurial heart and loves to build things. He's like that mate who, as soon as one DIY renovation is finished, is already planning the next. When the time came for Ronnie to walk away from UTV and Disney, there was perhaps a part of him that was exhilarated about the possibility of starting a new foundation and building something up again.

The other reason Ronnie managed to walk away with a sense of tranquility is because his life's ambition is greater than simply producing films, or building a larger business. Ronnie knew that, in channelling his passion into charity, building up others through education, he'd be able to find similar satisfaction. He might have been trading out the twin thrills of box-office receipts and accepting major film awards, but he could find equal satisfaction in helping others, at least on the massive scale he imagined.

I know my cricket career will come to an end one day. Either I'll call it, or my form will fade and it'll be time to go. I still have a few years in the game yet, but I like to think that when it's my time to move on I'll be able to find equal satisfaction in another area of my life, and perhaps that is to build something new and give something back in the same way that Ronnie has.

Ronnie's story is a reminder that it's important to have a vision that can change, adapt and also accommodate the present moment – to focus narrowly on the future you want, but not so narrowly that you miss the opportunities that appear in the present. After all, the present is the only time we're guaranteed.

# 10

## See the world as it is, not how you wish it was; love your kids that way too

*A conversation with Rob Sitch*

ROB SITCH IS A COMEDIAN, ACTOR, PRODUCER, DIRECTOR, golfer, mentor and mate – not necessarily in that order. First and foremost, though, he's a dad: five times over.

When I began putting this book together, Rob was one of the first people I approached, for a couple of reasons. When we play golf or get together on Zoom – which we do every month or so, where five of us chat through our current life or leadership challenges – I always find him to be funny and personable, wise and coherent. He's a fount of knowledge too, about most things, but especially about fatherhood.

A lot of my friends are dads, but most of them are just starting the ride, as I am. We relatively new dads are taking it one step at a time, constantly sniffing the air to try to tell whether something's on fire or not. Rob's five children are either adults or moving towards adulthood; he's not an empty nester yet, but he's certainly not changing nappies anymore.

I wanted to speak to Rob because he can talk about fatherhood with a bit of distance, and because of the kind of dad I know him to be. Rob's a great and attentive father, and he's also managed to maintain a high work output – he even managed to build a large company in a very competitive field while his kids were young. For at least a few years, I'll be juggling an intense, time-consuming career with fatherhood, and I hope to come out the other end of it like Rob, with a sense of fulfilment in my career and a happy family.

When I told Rob the reasons I wanted to speak to him, he told me, 'I'd love to say I had a plan, but I didn't. I will say this first: when you are a dad, you still can have everything in life. You just can't have it all at once anymore.'

*

There's a lot of TV and film that you might know Rob Sitch from. The best place to start is the first film he directed (which he also co-wrote and co-produced), *The Castle*.

For those who haven't seen it, *The Castle* is the story of a tow-truck driver, Darryl Kerrigan, who fights against the government's compulsory acquisition of his home, which sits right next to an airport. Darryl isn't a cultured man, but he's positive and good and kind, and he has a deep love of aviation and engineering. Despite being given the opportunity to sell up for a good price, he doesn't want to move. He loves living next to an airport, and also loves the powerlines that run across his property, because they 'are a reminder of man's ability to generate electricity'. He adds that the planes constantly flying overhead are probably why his house is worth 'almost as much today as when we bought it'.

There's a lot of wit, heart and wisdom in that film, and it has a lot of Rob's childhood in it too. The working-class simplicity of the Kerrigan family, and especially Darryl, probably doesn't resemble Rob's family, but he said the love and closeness of the nuclear family does, as well as the idea of a family being an insular unit. He didn't grow up next to an airport, but his cousins did, and as a ten-year-old, he thought those cousins were the luckiest people in the world. Like Darryl, Rob's father loved aviation and engineering, having been an astronavigator with a bomber crew in the Pacific during World War II.

Rob said his father and his father's friends, many of whom also flew in the war and recreationally, instilled a similar love of aviation in him. Young Rob became 'obsessive' about flying and wanted to be a Royal Australian Air Force pilot. Until he was fifteen, that was his only career plan – then, at an RAAF preselection testing day, Rob discovered he has a degree of colour blindness, meaning he would never be approved to fly a military aircraft.

Rob had to rethink his dreams, so decided to become a doctor. He enrolled in Medicine at the University of Melbourne, where he worked hard until his studies were hijacked by 'a hobby that got out of control'. 'At uni I figured I should try some things,' he said. 'By the age of twenty I'd never been on stage, so I auditioned for the Melbourne Uni dramatic society. I thought I did well.' In fact, Rob had not done well. When the cast list was posted on a bulletin board, his name was nowhere to be found. 'I ran into the guy who was the secretary of the dramatic society, and he goes, "Oh, a few people just missed out … Mind you, you weren't one of those either."' Rob laughed.

He persisted, though, and auditioned again the next year. This time his name was included in the cast list on the bulletin board, but in a non-speaking role. The role, he said, was the worst in the production, but he added that the camaraderie of theatre was something he instantly loved and it was an itch that couldn't be scratched.

When a friend in the cast ('he had the second-worst role') asked if Rob wanted to audition for the upcoming university comedy revue, Rob was in. In that revue, where the students had to produce, devise, write and perform their own sketches, Rob found a calling. He said the experience of being on stage and performing comedy was 'absolutely the best fun I've ever had'. 'It was a team,' he told me. 'Everyone depended on each other. It was nerve-racking. It helped me develop this little addiction.'

After that revue, Rob and some new performing friends decided to reconstitute the Melbourne Union Revue. This comedy institution had once given performers such as Barry Humphries and Max Gillies their first gigs, but had been dormant for some time. At the Melbourne Union Revue, Rob started meeting other undergraduate and amateur comedians. Some, like Santo Cilauro and Tom Gleisner, became lifelong collaborators.

The core of writers and performers from the Melbourne Union Revue started another comedy group called The D-Generation. That group became a household name in Australia after creating both television and radio shows. Although this was before my time, I've seen clips of The D-Generation online and can understand why they were such a big hit.

Despite The D-Generation becoming one of the most famous comedy groups in the country, and Rob being a significant part of the group, he said he still saw his work in comedy as nothing more than a diversion. At the time, there was no precedent for what The D-Generation was doing, and the work didn't seem to provide a path for any career. There were professional actors and stand-up comedians, but not general-purpose sketch performers who threw in a bit of improv and current-affairs commentary.

Throughout his time in The D-Generation, Rob continued his medical studies, except for a year in which he deferred them. 'I went to the Dean of Medicine and said, "Look, this is what I'm thinking,"' explaining that he wanted to take two semesters off so he could pour all of his energies into his comedy work, which he thought would be fleeting. 'I was expecting [the Dean] to say, "Look, you've got to get serious or get out." He goes, "Gee, that sounds like a lot of fun. Go do that and come back if you like." And so I did. And I always resolved to come back and finish my studies because I didn't want to muck him around.'

Dr Rob Sitch finished his medical studies and even did his internship as a doctor, but the comedy addiction was always there – and the popularity of the shows he and his friends were producing, writing, directing and performing in only snowballed. The D-Generation shows evolved into *The Late Show*, which was an even more successful comedy and current-affairs television show on the ABC. Afterwards Rob and *The Late Show* team pitched the ABC a scripted series set at a commercial television current-affairs show called *Frontline*. When *Frontline* was greenlit, Rob and his friends set up a company, first called Frontline Television Productions and later Working Dog Productions.

*Frontline* was a massive hit for Working Dog, which also produced a faux seventies cop show called *Funky Squad*, again for the ABC. After those successes, Working Dog produced its first feature film, *The Castle*, a partially biographical film co-written and directed by Rob.

The film was made for less than $1 million and took in more than ten times that, with DVD and rights sales further bolstering the bottom line. In a 2022 YouGov poll, *The Castle* was chosen as Australia's most popular film of all time.

After that film, Working Dog started making the hugely popular non-scripted light entertainment show *The Panel* for Channel Ten, as well as *Russell Coight's All Aussie Adventures*, also for Ten. Then Working Dog produced another film, again co-written and directed by Rob. This film was a paean to astronavigation. Called *The Dish*, it centred on Australia's involvement in relaying live video footage of Neil Armstrong's and Buzz Aldrin's historic first steps on the moon in 1969. The film was even more successful than *The Castle*, and was the highest-grossing film in Australia in 2000.

Rob said his life back then was full and hectic, with thoughts of scripts, locations, budgets and casting at the front of his mind. At the back of his mind there was the thought that, at some point, he should slow down and start a family. 'I was thinking, *Well, hey, that's okay. I'm still twenty-six.* Only I wasn't twenty-six, I was thirty-six. Gee, that flashed by.'

He said a decision had to be made. Being in your mid-thirties is not a do-or-die period for a man wanting to be a father – even one who wanted to be the father of a large family, as Rob did – but it was a do-or-die period for a man who had already found the person he wanted to spend his life with. 'I think that there's two clocks going in life. There's a male clock and a female clock, and that's just the reality of biology. Days can go forever, but years go in a blink. [I realised] you can't go another ten years because therefore you're harming the other person's life and plans. If I keep this up, it will never happen. It's not something that you can kick down the road forever.'

Some sacrifices needed to be made, by Rob and also by his wife, Jane Kennedy. She is an exceptional writer, producer, performer and casting director who had been as essential to the success of Working Dog as anyone.

\*

Rob Sitch and Jane Kennedy met when she came to work on *The D-Generation* breakfast radio show in Melbourne. After graduating from Genazzano, a well-known Melbourne Catholic girls' school where she was the school captain, Jane had started a degree in Arts at Melbourne University. Initially, she was hired by The D-Generation as a straight newsreader, tasked with collecting, writing and reading the news during breaks. But as Rob and the other D-Generation performers bantered with the newsreader, they discovered that she had a sharp wit and keen intellect, and would be a stellar addition to the group.

Jane established herself as a performer and writer within the group. She became well known in her own right, first on *The Late Show* as a core cast member, writer and producer, then on *Frontline* as acidic reporter Brooke Vandenberg. Jane was a founding member of Working Dog, and co-wrote and co-produced *The Castle* and *The Dish*. She also co-created *The Hollowmen*, *The Panel* and *Thank God You're Here*.

In 2001, Jane gave birth to her and Rob's first child, Mia, then the next year a son, Josh, then two years later, Max, and two years after that twin boys Bailey and Andy.

In Rob and Jane's first few years as parents, Working Dog's success boomed. The company produced *The Panel*, as well as licensing Irish and New Zealand versions of the show. It also launched *Thank God You're Here*, an improv-comedy show that was a success in Australia and then was licensed all across the world, with versions being broadcast in eighteen countries including the US, Canada, the UK, Spain, Russia and Germany.

Once they had kids, it wasn't possible for Rob and Jane to continue to work as they had before. They had some money and could afford a nanny, but Rob said they couldn't outsource their parenting: 'Kids are alive 168 hours a week. You can hire a nanny, well, that's 30 hours. For the other 130 hours the toddler is hellbent on killing themselves.' They didn't *want* to outsource their parenting either – they wanted to be present parents, meaning one of the pair needed to stay home while the children were small.

'It was foretold. We worked at the same company, so we instinctively knew how it was going to go.' Rob kept working, while Jane hit pause on her career. According to Rob, this agreement was made by both him and Jane.

It's a decision I understand well. In the cricket world, professional players and our partners often have to reconcile the nature of the work with the stresses and needs of starting a family. Sometimes, given the time and travel requirements of cricketers' careers, and the remuneration that we get, it makes sense for our partners to stop working for a bit if we want to have children. It may be unfair, and there may be a gendered aspect to the decision, but in my case, as in Rob's, it's the difference between being able to start a family or not. Rob believes that in order to make this relationship dynamic work, there has to be a genuine mutual respect for the things both parents are doing to give their kids everything they can.

Jane has since come back to work, writing books and producing films and television shows. From 2019 she also hosted a nationally broadcast radio show with Mick Molloy on Triple M, that she tearfully quit in 2021 to concentrate on parenting, saying on air: 'This year I have two university kids, I've got a VCE/HSC student, I've got two Year Nines, all living at home, and I thought I could juggle everything. You put a lot of effort into it, and I just felt I couldn't do a hundred per cent with the kids and with a radio show. Unfortunately these pesky five teenagers are going to have to come first. That is what's happened. I'm sorry, everyone, I've loved it. It's bloody overwhelming, and I want to do the right thing by my kids.'

Rob told me, 'Every parent sacrifices. Sometimes it looks like people are doing it all, but no one has it all. You can take solace in that if you like.'

*

Like Rob's kids, I grew up in a household with four siblings. I loved being part of a big family and living in a home of loving chaos. I only know what I know and lived how I lived, but I never wished for fewer brothers or sisters and never yearned for the relative quiet of the houses of my only-child mates. There was always someone to run around with, always someone to play cricket or netball with, someone to share my thoughts with, to compete against, to grow with. I cherish all of it: the fun and the mayhem and the camaraderie.

It was great for us kids, but it was an incredible amount of work for our parents. I have no doubt they wouldn't have had it any other way, but I also know there would have been so many moments when it all felt like a storm that wouldn't end. With the endless asks and needs and colds and dietary requirements and requests and practices and games and costs and everything that's required for one kid, let alone five, there must have been days and weeks – if not months and maybe even years – that felt overwhelming.

The effort required to raise us kids wasn't something I thought about much when I was growing up, but I've been thinking about it since I became a dad. When Becky was pregnant, I assumed – like a lot of modern parents – that parenting was going to be an addition to my life. I thought there'd still be cricket and friends and golf and my marriage and everything that was in my life before, as well as my son. That's not how it is.

The moment I saw Albie, a helpless little pink-red bundle in his mother's arms, I had a revelation: parenting is actually transformative. After the moment your first child is born, your whole life becomes focused through that one singular lens. When Albie was born, all I wanted to do was be a good dad for him.

Parenting is hard work – and yes, it requires sacrifice – but I feel deeply that it can't be all-encompassing. Life has to go on. Beyond the need to earn a living and continue to build a career, a parent has an obligation to model what a good life looks like: one that has ambition and balance, compassion and care for the community. If you want your children to have drive and passion, you need to have drive and passion yourself, and you have to show them that you do.

As soon as Albie was born, I knew my primary job from then on was to be his dad as well as a husband. That wasn't my only job, though. I was the vice-captain of the Australian T20 team then, and four days after Albie was born I had to fly to the United Arab Emirates for the T20 World Cup. During that tournament I first felt a pain that I've experienced on and off since: of being totally emotionally connected to Becky and Albie while not being physically connected to them.

It's a pain I'm still learning to deal with. I am doing it, though, because it's important to do everything I can in cricket, while I can still do it. I do this to help set our family up, to be challenged, to live without regrets and to establish the importance of seizing life's opportunities when they come, knowing cricket won't be forever. I don't get to socialise with my mates much anymore, and I can practically feel my golf handicap ballooning out every day. And yes, I do feel anxious sometimes that my old life's gone. But I think those feelings are just part of fatherhood. It invites dads like me to compare what we're losing against what has been gained, and it reminds us just how lucky we are.

The point I'm trying to make here is that while a desire to be a good parent was in me from the moment I welcomed my son into the world, I also stressed that I had no idea how to actually do it. I feel privileged that my siblings and I had attentive and hardworking parents, and use them as an example to follow even if they, at the same time, were feeling those stresses.

Sometimes I forget that. I forget it because, when I was young, parenting seemed easy enough for my dad, Peter. To me it seemed natural that he'd be feeding us, clothing us, entertaining and educating us, carting us around here and there, and sitting in the freezing cold or boiling heat as my sisters and brothers and I played sport. Of course, he did that stuff for all of us kids, right? He was Dad.

Now, as a dad myself, I have a different perspective. Parenting is hard work, but we're able to do it because, above anything else, we want our kids to live happy and productive lives. I know now that fatherhood was hard for my dad, but I also know now that good parenting is like good batting – the true effort is only known to the participant.

*

Rob told me, 'Glenn Robbins said once, "Our best work's done when we're hurting a bit." I think that's true of family life. It's true of lots of things. Always hurts to do something really, really well. I don't think it comes through cleverness, I think it comes through a bit of pain.'

Parenthood is pain. That's not something you'd put on a Father's Day card, but it's probably the truth.

Rob said there are no particularly easy patches on the fatherhood journey, but that the most painful period is the first few years of each child's life, when the kids 'literally do not have an off switch'. 'There's no sugar-coating the mayhem that is those early years,' he added. 'When the kids are small and wild, and everyone is at their wits' end.'

He told me that life was especially hard in the early years. 'When we do [work] projects, they become insanely intense, and so it's almost you just come home, eat, clean and then get up at 5 am and go again. Meals felt like rations then, thrown under the door.'

According to Rob, in many ways the early years are also the most exciting period of parenting, as it's when each kid's personality and passions are revealed. I'm seeing some of this in Albie already. I had a misconception that he would be largely the product of his environment and upbringing. That's true to a certain extent, but there's this other, unique part of my son that's just his.

When a kid's personality starts to reveal itself, one of the great parental battles begins: what the kid wants to do versus what we, the parents, want them to do.

'I think parents are more involved now,' Rob said, 'and I think people have a really strong sense of trying to … It's not that we're tiger mums or tiger dads, but there's a tiny little voice inside your head saying, "Are we giving our kids every opportunity?"' He told me that's a great instinct, but that the outcomes aren't necessarily going to be representative of the input. He thinks some emotions can be transferred down the generations – for instance, if your kids grow up in a household where kindness is championed and they are treated with kindness, it's more likely they'll end up being kind. He added that this is not so true of activities such as physics, cricket or violin. In his experience, you can force a kid to do pretty much anything right into their teen years, but 'for every ten kids sitting at a piano, practising, there are nine who are plotting their escape'.

I've seen this first-hand. When I was playing junior cricket, I assumed that the gun players in their early teens would do best in under-seventeens, under-nineteens and then seniors. That wasn't the case, though. Often the best junior players dropped off, stopped training, slowed down or quit altogether. It was almost always for the same reason, too: they lost the love, passion and drive you need to get over that hump between junior and senior cricket – when your body and skills are developing as you play against finished products, and when you're being smashed around the ground, or failing at the crease, or trying to come back from injuries.

So where does that good passion come from? And why do some kids choose cricket and not dance or whatever? Some of it's obviously their environment. Rob's first passion was aviation, and that surely had something to do with his dad and his dad's mates. With me, I wouldn't have ended up where I am if my brothers and dad hadn't been into the sport. But how did comedy and performing become parts of Rob's personality? And why are my brothers and sisters so different to one another, and have always been?

When you try to understand your kids, Rob told me, you have to recognise that their personalities are constructed from art, science and magic – and that sometimes you just have to stop asking and go with it. 'Young kids just wake up one day, and they discover a rugby ball or an AFL football and they want to sleep with it, then it never changes. Some of it is environment and then there are certain things that are just in your kids.'

I'm guessing that's one of the most enjoyable parts of parenting and one of the most important life lessons you pick up along the way. You can't control everything, you can't plan everything, and you have to love your kids the way they are, not the way you imagined they would be.

*

'I think parenting is a more demanding environment now, especially for dads,' said Rob, who added that, when he was a boy, the kids in his neighbourhood 'basically raised themselves'. 'The kids were sort of out the door as soon as they could reach the doorknob. They'd be off playing cricket, riding bikes and whatever. A lot of that's taken a hit, some for good reasons' – Rob said that, growing up, everyone knew a kid who had a brother or a cousin who'd had a serious accident or even died from a misadventure – 'and some for bad.'

Now, Rob said, dads are so much more involved throughout their children's lives. 'I reckon my dad visited the school twice in my life. There were no parent–son nights, speech night hadn't been invented, you didn't have to umpire under-nines cricket. School is more complex, work is more complex. Our expectations have kicked up a gear.'

Like everything, Rob said, there are good and bad aspects of the change, but the good of being closer to your children far outweighs the bad, which is basically the reality of how inconvenient, annoying and stressful kids – even those you love – can be. 'It's amazing how many times you have to drill an idea into a kid's head, especially boys, until they get it. But they do get it eventually. Most of the time.'

Rob said the thing he reckons dads have to understand is that they will always overestimate their ability to predict what their kids will feel, want and do. 'Take holidays, for instance. I got the kids to the Amalfi Coast once, and we got to this amazing view, and I'm like, *How good is this?* I turn around – they're playing *Tetris* behind me. One thing I know for certain about kids is that they don't give a shit about views.' He added that although he's taken his kids around the world, the holiday they enjoyed the most was to the Australian Pinball Museum in the Victorian town of Nhill, during which they stayed at Ballarat's Kryal Castle a hotel decorated to look like an Arthurian castle.

'So,' I asked Rob, 'if that's the case, how do I parent? How do you plan, knowing that few if any of your plans are going to be received the way you expect them to be received?'

Rob said the value of plans is sometimes the care you give to them, not the plan itself. 'Even when parents are under stress and things are really bad, I think the number one job is just to create an environment of love and kindness. The kids will kind of do the rest.'

*

I loved talking to Rob about fatherhood because he spoke honestly about how difficult and unpredictable but also rewarding kids are.

I worry about being a dad sometimes, and whether I'm doing it right. That stress only rose a few weeks after speaking to Rob, when Becky and I found out that our son Albie will have a sibling soon. We were both absolutely ecstatic about the news, obviously, but there are stresses too. There would now be twice as many ways for us to get parenthood wrong.

I'm sure some of what I spoke about with Rob might come across as arduous, but the mood of our conversation was actually one of excitement. My chat with Rob reinforced for me that fatherhood is an adventure – and the nature of adventure is that you don't know what's going to happen along the way, nor, sometimes, even the destination.

I love Rob's idea that kids are their own little souls, even from a very young age, and that our job as parents isn't to control them but to support them, fuel them and enrich them. When we're doing that, they'll be able to do the controlling themselves. I also love the notion that having kids means inviting something bigger into your life. Although having no idea how my kids are going to turn out is a terrifying prospect, I'm calmed by the knowledge that I'll always love them, and I'm exhilarated by the adventure that this uncertainty promises.

# 11

## If you want to go fast, go alone;
## if you want to go far, go together

*A conversation with Becky Cummins*

IF THERE'S ONE IDEA THAT'S BEEN CEMENTED WHILE writing this book it is that no one does anything alone. Nothing significant anyway. Every difficult endeavour is completed as part of a team, and many of the most impressive feats, be they in sport, business and politics or life, are done as part of a partnership.

It's a theme that's come through in interview after interview. Ronnie Screwvala would not have built UTV, his billion-dollar company, without his business partner and content expert Zarina Mehta, who later became his wife, by his side. For all of John Bertrand's incredible aptitude as a leader and skipper, he says that there was no way he would have won the America's Cup but for the fortune of meeting engineering genius Ben Lexcen. Dennis Lillee credits his whole career to his grandfather. John Moriarty and Charlie Perkins pushed each other in football and in their political understanding. Professor Rich Scolyer could not have achieved his success in immunotherapy without the expertise and trust of his research partner, Professor Georgina Long. The list goes on and on.

Throughout my cricketing life I've met dozens if not hundreds of players who seemed to have the same attributes that I had, and I have often wondered why I've managed to get ahead and not fall by the wayside. One part, I have talked about already, is certainly drive. Another important factor, however, has been the people around me.

Everyone at the top needs a partner, team or family that can teach, support, challenge, inspire or otherwise help them excel and the dynamic of every such relationship is unique. We are all limited in our own ways; we all have our own strengths, abilities and deficits. The best partnerships augment each other's strengths and mitigate their deficits, creating a capability beyond what any one person could muster alone. I know credit for my career isn't solely mine and I know one to whom I owe the lion's share of my success: my partner and wife, Becky.

Like most cricketers I've always believed in the power of partnerships. I don't know whether it's the camaraderie, the shared sense of purpose or complementary talent and style, but I've found good partnerships can create a force more powerful than the sum of the two players involved. This is true with bat and ball in hand. In listening to the stories of the people in this book, I'm confident also that this is a phenomenon that goes well beyond the pitch. So, there could be no more perfect an interview subject for the topic of partnerships than the one in my home already.

I credit so much of my life to Becky, and my career as a cricketer, and especially as a captain. For the handful of guys who play all three forms of the game – Steve Smith, Mitchell Starc and Josh Hazlewood come to mind – the eternal summer that catapults us around the globe can be exhilarating but also completely exhausting. Even over the course of writing this book, I've been in more than a dozen countries, and on the road for nine of the last twelve months.

It's a hell of a life and one I'd choose again a hundred times out of hundred, but I couldn't imagine staying at the top of the game for as long as I have without sharing it with someone who consistently supports and loves me but also inspires and challenges me, and teaches me how to be the leader, husband, father and man I want to be.

I've had some luck in my career, but none like the luck I found in Sydney's Kings Cross one night eleven years ago.

*

Becky was twenty-two years old when she came to Australia, like a lot of young Brits, on a working holiday. She was raised in Harrogate, North Yorkshire, the daughter of a former race-car driver and an optician. Having finished her undergraduate degree in English literature and doing a ski season in France, Becky had taken a job at a prison near to her home but wanted more from life than the Yorkshire spa town could provide. 'Harrogate is lovely,' she said, 'but it's just a bit insular. I wanted to get out and see some of the world.'

Meanwhile, I was twenty years old and I'd had a Cricket Australia contract for more than two years by then, but I'd barely played for Australia. I'd just received the news of a recurrence of my back stress fracture, essentially ruling me out cricket for 12 months. I had months of rehab ahead of me, and after that, who knew if I'd get back to the top level? It was feeling like my dream of a cemented spot in the Aussie side was going to be forever just beyond my grasp.

My situation felt hopeless, and I wanted to do something to break out of that. I'd completely dedicated myself to cricket at that point, which had come at a cost in other ways. I'd never gone out to a nightclub on a Sunday before, but after one of my brother's mates suggested it as just irresponsible enough, I said, *Screw it*, and off I went. It turned out to be one of the best decisions I ever made.

Through the basically empty night club, Becky and I caught each other's eyes. Our conversation that night was easy, like we'd known each other for ages.

As far as starts go, it was an excellent one.

I didn't tell Becky that I played cricket professionally at first, because I felt like a bit of a fraud, with my tenuous potential at the time far outweighing my actual experience. I just told her I was a student (which I was), doing a business and finance degree at the University of Technology, Sydney.

A couple of days later, Becky walked past a KFC and saw an image of me in the shopfront. She said, 'There you were on a poster, with a bucket on your head. I was like, *What's this guy I've started seeing doing in an ad?*'

She was mildly interested but quite unfazed by the cricket thing – hers was a family that didn't pay much attention to cricket and cricketers – and we continued to see each other for a couple of months, and we had a great summer together. Then summer came to an end.

Becky had always planned to go home after the summer, but she decided to stick around in Australia for a few more weeks to see what would happen. She said, 'I called my dad at the airport when I dropped my brother off and told him, "I'm not flying home. I'm going to stay with a friend." That was the moment I knew we were going to give it a go. I didn't know anyone else in Australia, so it was a bigger deal to me than it was to you.'

I hadn't thought much about that initial sacrifice she was making – I was twenty, immature, and had just started to come back to cricket as part of the Perth Scorchers Big Bash team. Becky came to Perth with me, and after the season I asked her to accompany me to the Allan Border Medal red carpet event. 'Your mum called me and told me I'd need a gown,' she said. 'When I got there I was in awe of it all.' Truth is, both of us felt like outsiders then. I'd hardly ever toured with those guys, and I felt far more *out* of the Aussie side than in.

Becky and I were caught in a whirlwind romance, but we both saw that we had to stop spinning at some point. 'I never wanted to be that girl who went to Australia and fell in love and never came back,' Becky said. And I was trying to be pragmatic. We were both trying not to become one of those long-distance relationships, where both people know it's not going to last. Five months after we met, Becky accepted an internship in Leeds, UK, and off she went back home. We didn't say it was final, but we went back to our normal lives with an eye to seeing how it played out.

\*

After Becky left Australia, I was busy, dedicated, and finally playing cricket – and yet, Becky was never far from my mind. When I did go out with my mates, I always had an eye on the UK time zone, waiting for her to wake so we could Facetime.

We were in contact every day, and met up a couple of times over an 18 month period. When I look back now, it seems crazy but then we were just taking every day as it came, and each day I wanted to keep in contact. Staying close always seemed to be the right thing to do, and we always wanted to know what the other was feeling and what they'd been doing, even thought we were only ever a day away from an update.

One day, Becky called me from the seat of her car and she was upset. She'd started a new job and, during the probation period that she'd hated, she'd decided to quit. She'd always felt like she should be in England, but in that moment she didn't know why.

'Why don't you just come back?' I asked.

It wasn't until later that I found out she'd been waiting quite a long time for me to pop that question.

*

They say timing is everything in life, and there's some truth to that. But there's also truth to accepting that, to a certain extent, you have to make your own timing. Opportunities will come your way, but they'll rarely come at the time of your choosing. An underrated aspect of success is being open to seizing opportunities that come at an inopportune time, as Elizabeth Day does.

This is also something Ronnie and I talked about, when we discussed his rise through the Indian media industry. A few times he'd mentioned serendipity, and I'd asked whether he defined it as some kind of cosmic or karmic gift. He said that, for him, it was instead the ability to see opportunities in unexpected places. 'It's a skill, really,' he said. I reckon it may even be two skills: the ability to recognise an opportunity when it's been presented, and the ability to do something about it.

Both skills have been demonstrated by a few of the people I've interviewed. Rob Sitch was a medical student, Dennis was an amateur cricketer and Julia Gillard was a lawyer with a background in student politics. The opportunities they were presented with were perhaps not those they had planned for. Indeed, it might have been easier for them to continue down the well-trodden paths before them. But they instead grabbed those unexpected opportunities with both hands and held tight, and in each instance, they changed their lives and their entire fields.

Part of how they did this was through passion. Passion is a powerful motivational force that can guide us and drive us, as it does Nedd Brockmann when he keeps putting one foot in front of the other. Passion is the 'bubbles in the water' that drove John Bertrand to win the America's Cup.

I was only twenty when I met Becky. Just as she had it stuck in her head that she was English, so too did I consider myself a cricketer first and foremost. I didn't want a distraction in my life then, but I didn't want to lose Becky either. That passion we had for each other changed the trajectory of our lives – and I reckon it will again and again.

*

Throughout 2016, I was studying at uni and rehabbing again.

I'd been working with Dennis on creating a sustainable bowling action and I was ready for some red-ball cricket, which I assumed would be some Shield matches. My hope was that I'd be able to use those matches to catapult myself into consideration for Ashes selection the next summer. Then Mitchell Starc was unexpectedly sidelined with an injury and I was recalled to play against India in the third Test in 2017.

Since Becky had come back to Sydney, I was pretty consistently home and we had established a lovely, homebound routine. Soon after arriving in Sydney, Becky found a job that she loved, and with my training finishing at 3pm, I had time to cook dinner, which often would be on the table when she came home. We spent all our nights together and our weekends were spent with family and friends. But then, as she said, 'You got a phone call one day and that was it. You were gone.'

Becky told me she feels like I've been away ever since. I feel that way sometimes too. 'Looking back, I'm really glad that I didn't know what our life would be like,' Becky said. 'At first, I really enjoyed the novelty of travelling, staying in beautiful hotels and taking time off work. Who wouldn't? It all sounds perfect on paper and don't get me wrong, we live the most amazing life. Cricket brings us enormous amounts of joy and I love the chaos that touring life brings. But as time went on, I realised that there were aspects to it that I hadn't fully prepared for.

'As I've gotten older, I've realised what's really important in life and that's not staying in hotels, no matter how nice they are. I am at my happiest when I'm at home surrounded by family, doing the things we mostly take for granted. The luxury of filling up my own fridge, sleeping in my own bed, having a weekly routine. The simple things are what I have learned mean everything in life for me.

'Living life away from home can be extremely lonely. I really miss having a friend pop over for a cup of tea, chatting to my local cafe owner or watching [Albie] ride his bike down the back lane. When I am home things can be tough too because, for about ten months of the year I am alone, and the person I most want to spend my days with is away.'

It's a life no-one really fully understands, not even our extended families. The sacrifice that our partners make to support our careers is to commit to a life of isolation. Whereas most travelling jobs involve pockets of time travelling, our lives are spent away, with small pockets of time at home. We're away from home for over three hundred days in a busy year. It's a life spent always adjusting to another time zone and another schedule, that's designed around the needs of someone else. With the cricket calendar being what it is, Becky and I are rarely in control of our own lives. That's fine for me, as when I hand over control of my time to the team, they hand me back an opportunity to fulfill my dreams. For Becky, it's a little bit different.

'As all parents know, becoming a mother brings a whole new purpose to life, but also challenges too,' Becky added. 'It's wonderful having a little buddy to travel with who you love, but infants aren't always the easiest travel companions. I have a very supportive family and we are privileged in many ways, and even with all that, it is still extremely difficult.'

I'm glad Becky spoke about the challenges becoming a parent brought, because not doing so dismisses her strength and achievement. Some days are especially hard on tour, and doubly so with the stress that travelling around with a young child brings. Yet she keeps going. Like Nedd on blistered feet, like Julia in the face of ad hominem attacks, Becky always has energy for the next hour, the next day and the next flight. I wondered how she does it.

'You have to be selfless, yet you have to really know your self-worth,' she answered.

Becky puts Albie's and my needs over her own every day.

\*

The hardest travel I ever did was without Becky, but while doing it I took on board a lesson she'd been trying to tell me for years. In 2021, after the world was slowing reanimating after COVID had frozen everything the first time, I went to India for an IPL season. The season ended prematurely after a wave of infections hit India, even piercing the biosecurity bubble our team was working within, and we were sent off for two sets of two-week quarantines: one allowing us to get on a plane heading to Australia then another allowing us to be free in the country.

It was tough, being away from Becky for that long, and while in the first quarantine, I received a call from my family that made the situation even more difficult. Doctors had found cancer in my mum's brain, and she was not expected to live much longer than Christmas. 'That's when things got really hard,' Becky said. 'I could feel how tough you were doing and there really wasn't anything I could do to help.'

I'm not ashamed to say that I struggled at times in those long days in quarantine, as so many Australians did. I learned a few things in those weeks, though, about the impermanence of life and the importance of each day.

Before then, I'd had this idea in my mind that I'd go through my cricketing career first and, afterwards, the rest of my life would happen. Becky was often reminding me otherwise. 'That's not how life works,' she said, in a lesson I would later reflect on when speaking with Shaun Christie-

David. 'There isn't any part of life that's just the path to the next part of life. It's all your life, it's all happening. You have to live all parts of your life now, because it's all happening now.'

She'd told me that many times. But sometimes it takes a low to reveal the truth of a lesson. It was only during that quarantine, then receiving that news about my mum, and afterwards, that I understood this one. It was painfully earned but very important.

*

Our first baby, Albie, was born October 2021 and I had to leave Becky and our son four days after the birth. A few weeks later, I was named Test captain. It was a difficult time, and one in which I felt immense pride for many reasons. As Becky says, 'We arrived home from the hospital on the day you left and I remember walking in on you sobbing on the floor while you were packing your bags. All I could think was: "Why is he so emotional? We are going to be fine. It's not a big deal." They say ignorance is bliss. When I look back, [looking after a newborn on my own for about a month] was the hardest thing I had ever done in my life at that point. But I got through each day knowing I would be on a plane soon and reunited with you, so I clung onto that. That alone got me through some very lonely and tiring days and nights. When I finally arrived in Brisbane in November for the start of the summer series, we had two blissful days together before Pat was made Test captain.

'It was an amazing thing to happen, and so deserved, but also it felt like my world had just crumbled. I had no control over anything. This baby was supposed to be the most important thing in our life, and all I wanted was for us to be together to enjoy him. It felt like that importance, and that time, was being torn away from me. [Your] new role was all anybody was talking about. It was all over the news. And every decision and every meeting relating to the captaincy seemed so pressing. I was so proud but also felt a bit hollow.

'You stepped up to the task and were absolutely amazing. I knew you were the best man for the job and this was your time to shine, but what absolutely shit timing. I often thought of how selfish it was for me to be thinking like that. I was only a few weeks postpartum and physically and mentally exhausted, but I will never forget the moment I realised that I just had to go home and do it alone. I had to, because if Albie and I stayed with him, it would break his heart and also his concentration. He couldn't be captain *and* a young father in that moment and I felt the best thing to do was to let him captain.'

I recognise now that it's only with Becky's love, strength and sacrifice that I can continue touring, playing and succeeding as I have been. Recognition and acknowledgement of the other's successes and sacrifices is at the heart of any good partnership. Thinking now about how I'd describe Becky's – which are largely for the benefit of others and go mostly unheralded – I think the right word to use is courage.

*

When I spoke with Nedd, he talked about the idea of 'showing up'. He said, for some showing up means pushing themselves to extremes to find their limits. For others, it is about applying themselves completely to their families, jobs or values. I don't think Becky intended to return home with Albie in order to push herself as Nedd does – though that ended up being the case! I think she did it because, for her, showing up has nothing to do with sport and everything to do with looking after those she cares about.

My experience with my mum, and now with Becky, is that some people excel at seeing to the heart of life. They see activities like sport and business as *part* of life, not life itself. As Shaun's mum told him, she didn't care how much money he was earning – she just wanted him to buy her a coffee every so often. This is a perspective that can not only help you as a person, but can also help you as an athlete and a leader. It's so often useful to step back, take a breath and see things in context. That's something I find far easier to do with Becky and Albie around.

'I think I can snap you out of things,' Becky tells me. 'Sometimes you're on your phone and you're stressed, and I know it's your job, but Albie's tapping you on your foot and he wants to show you a picture he's drawn. You can worry [too much] what people are going to say, and you're the sort of person that doesn't want to upset the apple cart.'

She's right. Throughout my career, I have been wary of doing things differently to the way they have been done before, or I have been too attentive of external voices, critics and the media, and even of my assumptions of what people are saying about my decisions. Letting go of that has been essential as a leader. As my conversations with Dennis Lillee and John Moriarty revealed to me, leaders must be able to fearlessly push the boundaries in service of what they feel is right, even when everyone around them is telling them to stay on the well-trodden path. You have to be true to your values, not just what a number on a scoreboard says. As a leader, you also have understand that values change and vary throughout the team you lead because the lives they have led will have been unlike yours.

My perspective on cricket is very different to how I once saw it. I still see it as a part of my life – an important part, but just a part. When I'm out on the pitch with the Australian team, I don't just see them as men in the middle of a cricket match but also men in the middle of their lives. As I am. I expect professionalism from everyone I work with, but I also try to understand their actions in the context of everything else happening in their lives.

Without Becky, and Albie and without living the life we've been leading together, I might have understood that idea in principle, but I don't think I would have embraced and lived it. And without living it, I wouldn't have been the right person to lead a team, especially not the Australian Test team.

*

Theres nothing quite like the first morning of a Test match. The grass is freshly mown, the lines on the pitch are being painted and the buzz around the ground is building. One of the real thrills of the start of any match is that the scoreboard always starts at 0–0, and no matter how many games you have played there is still a part of you thinking that anything can happen.

How do you ensure that the fear of the unknown doesn't debilitate you before a ball is even bowled? We all do this differently. Knowing I have prepared as best as I can helps. So does the confidence that comes through experience, and having a body of work that reminds me I have worked through just about any problem that will get thrown at me.

I also often find myself, in the leadup to a game, thinking about the past and the future. If I'm still nervous, I'll sometimes remind myself of that little boy playing in the backyard in the Blue Mountains and think about how thrilled he'd be to be facing this challenge. (Some days it's the opposite problem and I'll find I need a few nerves to motivate me to perform at my best. In that case, I'll still think about my past and let that dial up the excitement and push me out of feeling too relaxed.)

I'll also think about the future. About whether, in fifty years, I'll regret more the chances I took, or the ones I didn't. Either way, I know – just as I know the sun will still come up tomorrow – that I'll still have my health, my family and my friends, and I'll be okay.

Then I'll think, *If I'm still nervous, isn't that a good thing?* Nerves indicate that I really care about the outcome; that my passion for the game is still there. As John Bertrand said, to do extraordinary things, you have to be a bit screwed up. You have to have that abnormal passion. That often helps me to rationalise myself out of feeling nervous. If my nerves are going to help me, good! If they aren't, and the only thing I'm nervous about is failing, then what good are nerves going to do me in avoiding that failure? By looking backwards at my younger self and forwards towards my future, the past and future ground me in the present and the nerves fall away.

*

As I write the last few paragraphs of this book, I'm back home in Sydney. It's very early in the morning; Becky and Albie are still sleeping. I'm off soon to a group conditioning class at a gym in Bondi. I have a coffee in hand and the caffeine is supposed to be giving that little kick out the door but it's not working yet.

I've always wanted to play matches, but have never really loved training, especially strength and fitness training. I've always done it though, always managed to show up, even though my body and mind are telling me to do something else. I will get to this morning's class.

Before I started this book, I'd never really thought of resolve. It just isn't a word I'd normally use. But it encapsulates everything I've learned from this experience. When I think about resolve, it brings to mind longevity and consistency. Any time you have a set-back, it's that inner fortitude saying, 'Nup, I'm gonna get through this. Nothing is going to knock me around. I can solve this problem. I can bounce back from this. I can make the best of this bad situation. I know what direction I'm going in, and I can keep going.' It's a resolution to aim high, not play it safe and move the game on, go in the direction you've decided to go and not get knocked off course. And then to keep doing that day after day.

When I reflect on my career in cricket, the players who impress me the most are the ones who've been doing it for fifteen years or more, because you know nobody has had it all easy for that long. Those players have been knocked about so many times by injury, selection, poor form, but they always keep finding a way to come back. Someone can have an awesome season or two – heaps of people have that – but it's the long careers in cricket that impressed me. It's the same for all of the people I spoke to: they just keep showing up.

That's Test cricket as well. There's a physical aspect to it, where you've got to wake up every day and go again. Everyone might have something going on in their life – injury, niggles, whatever – but they still show up, they are still in the arena.

I always thought the reason I managed to get to those strength and fitness sessions was because I wanted to be a better cricketer and because it's just part of the job. I now know that's probably not quite right. I train because I want to fulfill my potential as a person, and currently cricket is where a large part of that potential lies. In a few years' time, that won't be the case. There'll be some other endeavour and some other field that I'll be applying myself to, and there will be some aspect of that field that I won't love but will do anyway.

One thing I've taken away from this book, while speaking to these incredible people, is that leadership and achievement aren't goals, they are by-products. You achieve because of the person you choose to be, you're not the person you are because you've achieved.

I don't think Julia strove to become prime minister, John to win the America's Cup, or Rich to cure cancer. They strove to become people who *could* do those things, and they would have been as outstanding in any field they set their minds to.

That's the case for me too, but it wasn't always. As a younger man I just wanted to reach cricket's peaks. But now my goals are different. I still want to be a great cricketer, but it's just as important to me that I be a great dad, husband, son, friend, captain and maybe mentor too.

As a younger man I might have thought different skills were required to be all of those things and that other goals might take me away from the main goal. Now I know that's not true.

Those goals beyond cricket are intertwined with my life with Becky, and I credit her for the idea that I have to be the same man on the field, at home, at the pub and in the media. If I am the same man everywhere, then my resolve in any field will travel, through space and time. I'm a cricketer today, and tomorrow I'll be something else, but with the ability to tap into all of the experiences I've had.

I *am* a cricketer today though, and with the dawn finally breaking and my coffee cup empty, it's time to train.